THE ONLY REVOLUTION

THE ONLY REVOLUTION

by

J. KRISHNAMURTI

Edited by Mary Lutyens

PERENNIAL LIBRARY

Harper & Row, Publishers

New York, Hagerstown, San Francisco, London

A hardcover edition of this book is published by Harper &
Row, Publishers, Inc.

First PERENNIAL LIBRARY edition published 1977

ISBN: 0–06–080410–6

77 78 79 80 5 4 3 2 1

CONTENTS

INDIA

I

MEDITATION IS NOT an escape from the world; it is not an isolating self-enclosing activity, but rather the comprehension of the world and its ways. The world has little to offer apart from food, clothes and shelter, and pleasure with its great sorrows.

Meditation is wandering away from this world; one has to be a total outsider. Then the world has a meaning, and the beauty of the heavens and the earth is constant. Then love is not pleasure. From this all action begins that is not the outcome of tension, contradiction, the search for self-fulfilment or the conceit of power.

The room overlooked a garden, and thirty or forty feet below was the wide, expansive river, sacred to some, but to others a beautiful stretch of water open to the skies and to the glory of the morning. You could always see the other bank with its village and spreading trees, and the newly planted winter wheat. From this room you could see the morning star, and the sun rising gently over the trees; and the river became the golden path for the sun.

At night the room was very dark and the wide window showed the whole southern sky, and into this room one night came—with a great deal of fluttering—a bird. Turning on the light and getting out of bed one saw it under the bed. It was an owl. It was about a foot-and-a-half high with extremely wide big eyes and a fearsome beak. We gazed at each other quite close, a few feet apart. It was frightened by the light and the closeness of a human being. We looked at each other without blinking for quite a while, and it never lost its height and its fierce dignity. You could see the cruel claws, the light feathers and the wings tightly held against the body. One would have liked to touch it, stroke it, but it would not have allowed that. So presently the light was turned out and for some time there was quietness in the room. Soon there was a fluttering of the wings—you could feel the air against your face—and the owl had gone out of the window. It never came again.

It was a very old temple; they said it might be over three thousand years old, but you know how people exaggerate. It certainly was old; it had been a Buddhist temple and about seven centuries ago it became a Hindu temple and in place of the Buddha they had put a Hindu idol. It was very dark inside and it had a strange atmosphere. There were pillared halls, long corridors carved most beautifully, and there was the smell of bats and of incense.

The worshippers were straggling in, recently bathed, with folded hands, and they walked around these corridors, prostrating each time they passed the image, which was clothed in bright silks. A priest in the innermost shrine was chanting and it was nice to hear well-pronounced Sanskrit. He wasn't in a hurry, and the words came out easily and gracefully from the depths of the temple. There were children there, old ladies, young men. The professional people had put away their European trousers and coats and put on dhotis, and with folded hands and bare shoulders they were, with great devotion, sitting or standing.

And there was a pool full of water—a sacred pool—with many steps leading down to it and pillars of carved rock around it. You came into the temple from the dusty road full of noise and bright, sharp sunshine, and in here it was very shady, dark and peaceful. There were no candles, no kneeling people about, but only those who made their pilgrimage around the shrine, silently moving their lips in some prayer.

A man came to see us that afternoon. He said he was a believer in Vedanta. He spoke English very well for he had been educated in one of the universities and had a bright, sharp intellect. He was a lawyer, earning a great deal of money, and his keen eyes looked at you speculatively, weighing, and somewhat anxious. He appeared to have read a great deal, including something of western theology. He was a middle-aged man, rather thin and tall, with the dignity of a lawyer who had won many cases.

He said: "I have heard you talk and what you are saying is pure Vedanta, brought up to date but of the ancient tradition." We asked him what he meant by Vedanta. He replied: "Sir, we postulate that there is only Brahman who creates the world and the illusion of it, and the Atman—which is in every human being—is of that Brahman. Man has to awaken from this everyday consciousness of plurality and the manifest world, much as he would awaken from a dream. Just as this dreamer creates the totality of his dream so the individual consciousness creates the totality of the manifest world and other people. You, sir, don't say all this but surely you mean all this for you have been born and bred in this country and, though you have been abroad most of your life, you are part of this ancient tradition. India has produced you, whether you like it or not; you are the product of India and you have an Indian mind. Your gestures, your statue-like stillness when you talk, and your very looks are part of this ancient heritage. Your teaching is surely the continuation of what our ancients have taught since time immemorial."

Let us brush aside whether the speaker is an Indian

brought up in this tradition, conditioned in this culture, and whether he is the summation of this ancient teaching. First of all he is not an Indian, that is to say, he does not belong to this nation or to the community of Brahmins, though he was born in it. He denies the very tradition with which you invest him. He denies that his teaching is the continuity of the ancient teachings. He has not read any of the sacred books of India or of the West because they are unnecessary for a man who is aware of what is going on in the world—of the behaviour of human beings with their endless theories, with the accepted propaganda of two thousand or five thousand years which has become the tradition, the truth, the revelation.

To such a man who denies totally and completely the acceptance of the word, the symbol with its conditioning, to him truth is not a second-hand affair. If you had listened to him, sir, he has from the very beginning said that any acceptance of authority is the very denial of truth, and he has insisted that one must be outside all culture, tradition and social morality. If you had listened, then you would not say that he is an Indian or that he is continuing the ancient tradition in modern language. He totally denies the past, its teachers, its interpreters, its theories and its formulas.

Truth is never in the past. The truth of the past is the ashes of memory; memory is of time, and in the dead ashes of yesterday there is no truth. Truth is a living thing, not within the field of time.

So, having brushed all that aside, we can now take up the central issue of Brahman, which you postulate. Surely, sir, the very assertion is a theory invented by an imaginative mind—whether it be Shankara or the modern scholarly theologian. You can experience a theory and say that it is so, but that is like a man who has been brought up and conditioned in the Catholic world having visions of Christ. Obviously such visions are the projection of his own conditioning; and those who have been brought up in the tradition of Krishna have experiences and visions born of their culture. So experience does not prove a thing. To recognise the vision as Krishna or Christ is the outcome of conditioned knowledge; therefore it is not real at all but a fancy, a myth, strengthened through experience and utterly invalid. Why do you want a theory at all, and why do you postulate any belief? This constant assertion of belief is an indication of fear—fear of everyday life, fear of sorrow, fear of death and of the utter meaninglessness of life. Seeing all this you invent a theory and the more cunning and erudite the theory the more weight it has. And after two thousand or ten thousand years of propaganda that theory invariably and foolishly becomes "the truth".

But if you do not postulate any dogma, then you are face to face with what actually is. The "what is", is thought, pleasure, sorrow and the fear of death. When you understand the structure of your daily living—with its competition, greed, ambition and the search for power—then you will see not only the absurdity of theories, saviours and gurus, but you may find an ending to sorrow, an ending to the whole structure which thought has put together.

The penetration into and the understanding of this structure is meditation. Then you will see that the world is not an illusion but a terrible reality which man, in his relationship with his fellow man, has constructed. It is this which has to be understood and not your theories of Vedanta, with the rituals and all the paraphernalia of organised religion.

When man is free, without any motive of fear, of envy or of sorrow, then only is the mind naturally peaceful and still. Then it can see not only the truth in daily life from moment to moment but also go beyond all perception; and therefore there is the ending of the observer and the observed, and duality ceases.

But beyond all this, and not related to this struggle, this vanity and despair, there is—and this is not a theory—a stream that has no beginning and no end; a measureless movement that the mind can never capture.

When you hear this, sir, obviously you are going to make a theory of it, and if you like this new theory you will propagate it. But what you propagate is not the truth. The truth is only when you are free from the ache, anxiety and aggression which now fill your heart and mind. When you see all this and when you come upon that benediction called love, then you will know the truth of what is being said.

2

What is important in meditation is the quality of the mind and the heart. It is not what you achieve, or what you say you attain, but rather the quality of a mind that is innocent and vulnerable. Through negation there is the positive state. Merely to gather, or to live in, experience, denies the purity of meditation. Meditation is not a means to an end. It is both the means and the end. The mind can never be made innocent through experience. It is the negation of experience that brings about that positive state of innocency which cannot be cultivated by thought. Thought is never innocent. Meditation is the ending of thought, not by the meditator, for the meditator is the meditation. If there is no meditation, then you are like a blind man in a world of great beauty, light and colour.

Wander by the seashore and let this meditative quality come upon you. If it does, don't pursue it. What you pursue will be the memory of what it was—and what was is the

death of what is. Or when you wander among the hills, let
everything tell you the beauty and the pain of life, so that
you awaken to your own sorrow and to the ending of it.
Meditation is the root, the plant, the flower and the fruit.
It is words that divide the fruit, the flower, the plant and the
root. In this separation action does not bring about goodness :
virtue is the total perception.

It was a long shady road with trees on both sides—a
narrow road that wound through the green fields of glisten-
ing, ripening wheat. The sun made sharp shadows, and the
villages on both sides of the road were dirty, ill-kept and
poverty-ridden. The older people looked ill and sad, but the
children were shouting and playing in the dust and throwing
stones at the birds high up in the trees. It was a very pleasant cool morning and a fresh breeze was blowing over the
hills.

The parrots and the mynahs were making a great deal of
noise that morning. The parrots were hardly visible among
the green leaves of the trees; in the tamarind they had several
holes which were their home. Their zig-zag flight was always
screechy and raucous. The mynahs were on the ground,
fairly tame. They would let you come quite near them before
they flew away. And the golden fly-catcher, the green and
golden bird, was on the wires across the road. It was a
beautiful morning and the sun was not too hot yet. There
was a benediction in the air and there was that peace before
man wakes up.

On that road a horse-drawn vehicle with two wheels and
a platform with four posts and an awning was passing by.
On it, stretched across the wheels, wrapped up in a white
and red cloth, was a dead body being carried to the river
to be burnt on its banks. There was a man sitting beside the
driver, probably a relative, and the body was jolting up and

down on that not too smooth road. They had come from some distance for the horse was sweating, and the dead body had been shaking all the way and it seemed to be quite rigid.

The man who came to see us later that day said he was a gunnery instructor in the navy. He had come with his wife and two children and he seemed a very serious man. After salutations he said that he would like to find God. He was not too articulate, probably he was rather shy. His hands and face looked capable but there was a certain hardness in his voice and look—for, after all, he was an instructor in the ways of killing. God seemed to be so remote from his everyday activities. It all seemed so weird, for here was a man who said he was in earnest in his search for God and yet his livelihood forced him to teach others the art of killing.

He said he was a religious man and had wandered through many schools of different so-called holy men. He was dissatisfied with them all, and now he had taken a long journey by train and bus to come and see us for he wanted to know how to come upon that strange world which men and saints have sought. His wife and children sat very silent and respectful, and on a branch just outside the window sat a dove, light brown, softly cooing to itself. The man never looked at it, and the children with their mother sat rigid, nervous and unsmiling.

You can't find God; there is no way to it. Man has invented many paths, many religions, many beliefs, saviours and teachers whom he thinks will help him to find the bliss that is not passing. The misery of search is that it leads to some fancy of the mind, to some vision which the mind has projected and measured by things known. The love which he seeks is destroyed by the way of his life. You cannot have a gun in one hand and God in the other. God is only a symbol, a word, that has really lost its meaning, for the

churches and places of worship have destroyed it. Of course,
if you don't believe in God you are like the believer; both
suffer and go through the sorrow of a short and vain life; and
the bitterness of every day makes life a meaningless thing.
Reality is not at the end of the stream of thought, and the
empty heart is filled by the words of thought. We become
very clever, inventing new philosophies, and then there is the
bitterness of their failure. We have invented theories about
how to reach the ultimate, and the devotee goes to the
temple and loses himself in the imaginations of his own mind.
The monk and the saint do not find that reality for both are
part of a tradition, of a culture, that accepts them as being
saints and monks.

The dove has flown away, and the beauty of the mountain
of cloud is upon the land—and truth is there, where you
never look.

3

It was an old Mogul garden with many great trees. There
were big monuments, dark inside with marble sepulchres,
and the rain and the weather had made the stone dark and
the domes still darker. There were hundreds of pigeons on
these domes. They and the crows would fight for a place,
and lower down on the dome were the parrots, coming
from everywhere in groups. There were nicely kept lawns,
well trimmed and watered. It was a quiet place and surprisingly there were not too many people. Of an evening the
servants of the neighbourhood with their bicycles would
gather on a lawn to play cards. It was a game they understood, but an outsider looking on couldn't make head or tail
of it. There were parties of children playing on a lawn of a
different tomb.

There was one tomb which was especially grand, with great arches, well proportioned, and a wall behind it which was asymmetrical. It was made of bricks and the sun and the rain had made it dark, almost black. There was a notice not to pick flowers but nobody seemed to pay much attention to it for they picked them all the same.

There was an avenue of eucalyptus, and behind it a rose garden with crumbling walls around it. This garden, with magnificent roses, was kept beautifully, and the grass was always green and freshly cut. Few people seemed to come to this garden and you could walk around it in solitude, watching the sun set behind the trees and behind the dome of the tomb. Especially in the evening, with the long dark shadows, it was very peaceful there, far from the noise of the town, from the poverty, and the ugliness of the rich. There were gypsies uprooting the weeds from the lawn. It was altogether a beautiful place—but man was gradually spoiling it.

There was a man sitting cross-legged in one of the remote corners of the lawn, his bicycle beside him. He had closed his eyes and his lips were moving. He was there for more than half an hour in that position, completely lost to the world, to the passers-by and to the screech of the parrots. His body was quite still. In his hands there was a rosary covered by a piece of cloth. His fingers were the only movement that one could see, apart from his lips. He came there daily towards the evening, and it must have been after his day's work. He was rather a poor man, fairly well fed, and he always came to that corner and lost himself. If you asked him he would tell you that he was meditating, repeating some prayer or some mantra—and to him that was good enough. He found in it solace from the everyday monotony of life. He was alone on the lawn. Behind him was a flowering jasmine; a great many flowers were on the ground, and the beauty of the moment lay around him. But he never saw that beauty for he was lost in the beauty of his own making.

Meditation is not the repetition of the word, nor the experiencing of a vision, nor the cultivating of silence. The bead and the word do quieten the chattering mind, but this is a form of self-hypnosis. You might as well take a pill.

Meditation is not wrapping yourself in a pattern of thought, in the enchantment of pleasure. Meditation has no beginning, and therefore it has no end.

If you say: "I will begin today to control my thoughts, to sit quietly in the meditative posture, to breathe regularly" —then you are caught in the tricks with which one deceives oneself. Meditation is not a matter of being absorbed in some grandiose idea or image: that only quietens one for the moment, as a child absorbed by a toy is for the time being quiet. But as soon as the toy ceases to be of interest, the restlessness and the mischief begin again. Meditation is not the pursuit of an invisible path leading to some imagined bliss. The meditative mind is seeing—watching, listening, without the word, without comment, without opinion— attentive to the movement of life in all its relationships throughout the day. And at night, when the whole organism is at rest, the meditative mind has no dreams for it has been awake all day. It is only the indolent who have dreams; only the half-asleep who need the intimation of their own states. But as the mind watches, listens to the movement of life, the outer and the inner, to such a mind comes a silence that is not put together by thought.

It is not a silence which the observer can experience. If he does experience it and recognise it, it is no longer silence. The silence of the meditative mind is not within the borders of recognition, for this silence has no frontier. There is only silence—in which the space of division ceases.

The hills were being carried by the clouds and the rain was polishing the rocks, big boulders that were scattered over the hills. There was a streak of black in the grey granite, and that morning this dark basalt rock was being washed by the rain and was becoming blacker.

The ponds were filling up and the frogs were making deep-throated noises. A whole group of parrots was coming in from the fields for shelter and the monkeys were scrambling up the trees, and the red earth became darker.

There is a peculiar silence when it rains, and that morning in the valley all the noises seemed to have stopped—the noises of the farm, the tractor and the chopping of wood. There was only the dripping from the roof, and the gutters were gurgling.

It was quite extraordinary to feel the rain on one, to get wet to the skin, and to feel the earth and the trees receive the rain with great delight; for it hadn't rained for some time, and now the little cracks in the earth were closing up. The noises of the many birds were made still by the rain; the clouds were coming in from the east, dark, heavily laden, and were being drawn towards the west; the hills were being carried by them, and the smell of the earth was spreading into every corner. All day it rained.

And in the stillness of the night the owls hooted to each other across the valley.

He was a school-teacher, a Brahmin, with a clean dhoti. He was bare footed and wore a western shirt. He was clean, sharp-eyed, apparently gentle in manner, and his salutation was a show of this humility. He was not too tall, and spoke English quite well, for he was an English teacher in town.

He said he didn't earn much, and like all teachers through-out the world he found it very difficult to make both ends meet. Of course he was married, and had children, but he seemed to brush all that aside as though it did not matter at all. He was a proud man, with that peculiar pride, not of achievement, not the pride of the well-born or of the rich, but that pride of an ancient race, of the representative of an ancient tradition and system of thought and morality which, actually, had nothing whatever to do with what he really was. His pride was in the past which he represented, and his brushing aside of the present complications of life was the gesture of a man who considers it all inevitable-but-so-un-necessary. His diction was of the south, hard and loud. He said he had listened to the talks, here under the trees, for many years. In fact his father had brought him when he was a young man, still at college. Later, when he got his present miserable job, he came every year.

"I have listened to you for many years. Perhaps I under-stand intellectually what you are saying but it doesn't seem to penetrate very deeply. I like the setting of the trees under which you talk, and I look at the sunset when you point it out—as you so often do in your talks—but I cannot *feel* it, I cannot touch the leaf and feel the joy of the dancing shadows on the ground. I have no feelings at all, in fact. I have read a great deal, naturally, both English literature and the literature of this country. I can recite poems, but the beauty which lies beyond the word has escaped me. I am becoming harder, not only with my wife and children but with everybody. In the school I shout more. I wonder why I have lost the delight in the evening sun—if I ever had it! I wonder why I no longer feel strongly about any of the evils that exist in the world. I seem to see everything intellec-tually and can reason quite well—at least I think I can—with almost anybody. So why is there this gap between the intellect and the heart? Why have I lost love, and the feeling of genuine pity and concern?"

Look at that bougainvilia out of the window. Do you see it at all? Do you see the light on it, its transparency, the colour, the shape and the quality of it?

"I look at it, but it means absolutely nothing to me. And there are millions like me. So I come back to this question— why is there this gap between the intellect and the feelings?"

Is it because we have been badly educated, cultivating only memory and, from earliest childhood, have never been shown a tree, a flower, a bird, or a stretch of water? Is it because we have made life mechanical? Is it because of this over-population? For every job there are thousands who want it. Or is it because of pride, pride in efficiency, pride of race, the pride of cunning thought? Do you think that's it?

"If you're asking me if I'm proud—yes I am."

But that is only one of the reasons why the so-called intellect dominates. Is it because words have become so extraordinarily important and not what is above and beyond the word? Or is it because you are thwarted, blocked in various ways, of which you may not be conscious at all? In the modern world the intellect is worshipped and the more clever and cunning you are the more you get on.

"Perhaps it may be all these things, but do they matter much? Of course we can go on endlessly analysing, describing the cause, but will that bridge the gap between the mind and the heart? That's what I want to know. I have read some of the psychological books and our own ancient literature but it doesn't set me on fire, so now I have come to you, though perhaps it may be too late for me."

Do you really care that the mind and heart should come together? Aren't you really satisfied with your intellectual capacities? Perhaps the question of how to unite the mind and the heart is only academic? Why do you bother about

bringing the two together? This concern is still of the intellect and doesn't spring, does it, from a real concern at the
decay of your feeling, which is part of you? You have divided
life into the intellect and the heart and you intellectually
observe the heart withering away and you are verbally concerned about it. Let it wither away! Live only in the intellect. Is that possible?

"I do have feelings."

But aren't those feelings really sentimentality, emotional
self-indulgence? We are not talking about that, surely. We
are saying: *Be* dead to love; it doesn't matter. Live entirely
in your intellect and in your verbal manipulations, your cunning arguments. And when you do actually live there—what
takes place? What you are objecting to is the destructiveness
of that intellect which you so worship. The destructiveness
brings a multitude of problems. You probably see the effect
of the intellectual activities in the world—the wars, the competition, the arrogance of power—and perhaps you are
frightened of what is going to happen, frightened of the
hopelessness and despair of man. So long as there is this
division between the feelings and the intellect, one dominat-
ing the other, the one must destroy the other; there is no
bridging the two. You may have listened for many years to
the talks, and perhaps you have been making great efforts
to bring the mind and the heart together, but this effort is
of the mind and so dominates the heart. Love doesn't belong
to either, because it has no quality of domination in it. It
is not a thing put together by thought or by sentiment. It is
not a word of the intellect or a sensuous response. You say,
"I must have love, and to have it I must cultivate the
heart". But this cultivation is of the mind and so you keep
the two always separate; they cannot be bridged or brought
together for any utilitarian purpose. Love is at the beginning,
not at the end of an endeavour.

"Then what am I to do?"

Now his eyes were becoming brighter; there was a movement in his body. He looked out of the window, and he was slowly beginning to catch fire.

You can't do anything. Keep out of it! And listen; and see the beauty of that flower.

4

Meditation is the unfolding of the new. The new is beyond and above the repetitious past—and meditation is the ending of this repetition. The death that meditation brings about is the immortality of the new. The new is not within the area of thought, and meditation is the silence of thought.

Meditation is not an achievement, nor is it the capture of a vision, nor the excitement of sensation. It is like the river, not to be tamed, swiftly running and overflowing its banks. It is the music without sound; it cannot be domesticated and made use of. It is the silence in which the observer has ceased from the very beginning.

The sun wasn't up yet; you could see the morning star through the trees. There was a silence that was really extraordinary. Not the silence between two noises or between two notes, but the silence that has no reason whatsoever—the silence that must have been at the beginning of the world. It filled the whole valley and the hills.

The two big owls, calling to each other, never disturbed that silence, and a distant dog barking at the late moon was part of this immensity. The dew was especially heavy, and as the sun came up over the hill it was sparkling with many colours and with the glow that comes with the sun's first rays.

The delicate leaves of the jacaranda were heavy with

dew, and birds came to have their morning baths, fluttering their wings so that the dew on those delicate leaves filled their feathers. The crows were particularly persistent; they would hop from one branch to another, pushing their heads through the leaves, fluttering their wings and preening themselves. There were about half-a-dozen of them on that one heavy branch, and there were many other birds, scattered all over the tree, taking their morning bath.

And this silence spread, and seemed to go beyond the hills. There were the usual noises of children shouting, and laughter; and the farm began to wake up.

It was going to be a cool day, and now the hills were taking on the light of the sun. They were very old hills—probably the oldest in the world—with oddly shaped rocks that seemed to be carved out with great care, balanced one on top of the other; but no wind or touch could loosen them from this balance.

It was a valley far removed from towns, and the road through it led to another village. The road was rough and there were no cars or buses to disturb the ancient quietness of this valley. There were bullock carts, but their movement was a part of the hills. There was a dry river bed that only flowed with water after heavy rains, and the colour was a mixture of red, yellow and brown; and it, too, seemed to move with the hills. And the villagers who walked silently by were like the rocks.

The day wore on and towards the end of the evening, as the sun was setting over the western hills, the silence came in from afar, over the hills, through the trees, covering the little bushes and the ancient banyan. And as the stars became brilliant, so the silence grew into great intensity; you could hardly bear it.

The little lamps of the village were put out, and with sleep the intensity of that silence grew deeper, wider and incredibly over-powering. Even the hills became more quiet, for they, too, had stopped their whisperings, their movement, and seemed to lose their immense weight.

She said she was forty-five; she was carefully dressed in a sari, with some bangles on her wrists. The older man with her said he was her uncle. We all sat on the floor overlooking a big garden with a banyan tree, a few mango trees, the bright bougainvilia and the growing palms. She was terribly sad. Her hands were restless and she was trying to prevent herself from bursting into speech and perhaps tears. The uncle said : "We have come to talk to you about my niece. Her husband died a few years ago, and then her son, and now she can't stop crying and has aged terribly. We don't know what to do. The usual doctors' advice doesn't seem to work, and she seems to be losing contact with her other children. She's getting thinner. We don't know where all this is going to end, and she insisted that we should come to see you."

"I lost my husband four years ago. He was a doctor and died of cancer. He must have hidden it from me, and only in the last year or so did I know about it. He was in agony although the doctors gave him morphine and other sedatives. Before my eyes he withered away and was gone."

She stopped, almost choking with tears. There was a dove sitting on the branch, quietly cooing. It was brownish-grey, with a small head and a large body—not too large, for it was a dove. Presently it flew off and the branch was swinging up and down from the pressure of its flight.

"I somehow cannot bear this loneliness, this meaningless existence without him. I loved my children; I had three of them, a boy and two girls. One day last year the boy wrote to me from school that he was not feeling well, and a few days later I got a telephone call from the headmaster, saying that he was dead."

Here she began to sob uncontrollably. Presently she produced a letter from the boy in which he had said that he wanted to come home for he was not feeling well, and that he hoped she was all right. She explained that he had been concerned about her; he hadn't wanted to go to school but had wanted to remain with her. And she more or less forced him to go, afraid that he would be affected by her grief. Now it was too late. The two girls, she said, were not fully aware of all that had happened for they were quite young. Suddenly she burst out: "I don't know what to do. This death has shaken the very foundations of my life. Like a house, our marriage was carefully built on what we considered a deep foundation. Now everything is destroyed by this enormous event."

The uncle must have been a believer, a traditionalist, for he added: "God has visited this on her. She has been through all the necessary ceremonies but they have not helped her. I believe in reincarnation, but she takes no comfort in it. She doesn't even want to talk about it. To her it is all meaningless and we have not been able to give her any comfort."

We sat there in silence for some time. Her handkerchief was now quite wet; a clean handkerchief from the drawer helped to wipe away the tears on her cheeks. The red bougainvilia was peeping through the window, and the bright southern light was on every leaf.

Do you want to talk about this seriously—go to the root of it all? Or do you want to be comforted by some explanation, by some reasoned argument, and be distracted from your sorrow by some satisfying words?

She replied: "I'd like to go into it deeply, but I don't know whether I have the capacity or the energy to face what you are going to say. When my husband was alive we used to come to some of your talks; but now I may find it very difficult to go along with you."

Why are you in sorrow? Don't give an explanation, for that will only be a verbal construction of your feeling, which will not be the actual fact. So, when we ask a question, please don't answer it. Just listen, and find out for yourself. Why is there this sorrow of death—in every house, rich and poor, from the most powerful in the land to the beggar? Why are you in sorrow? Is it for your husband—or is it for yourself? If you are crying for him, can your tears help him? He has gone irrevocably. Do what you will, you will never have him back. No tears, no belief, no ceremonies or gods can ever bring him back. It is a fact which you have to accept; you can't do anything about it. But if you are crying for yourself, because of your loneliness, your empty life, because of the sensual pleasures you had and the companionship, then you are crying, aren't you, out of your own emptiness and out of self-pity? Perhaps for the first time you are aware of your own inward poverty. You have invested in your husband, haven't you, if we may gently point it out, and it has given you comfort, satisfaction and pleasure? All you are feeling now—the sense of loss, the agony of loneliness and anxiety—is a form of self-pity, isn't it? Do look at it. Don't harden your heart against it and say: "I love my husband, and I wasn't thinking a bit about myself. I wanted to protect him, even though I often tried to dominate him; but it was all for his sake and there was never a thought for myself." Now that he has gone you are realising, aren't you, your own actual state? His death has shaken you and shown you the actual state of your mind and heart. You may not be willing to look at it; you may reject it out of fear, but if you observe a little more you will see that you are crying out of your own loneliness, out of your inward poverty—which is, out of self-pity.

"You are rather cruel, aren't you, sir?" she said. "I have come to you for real comfort, and what are you giving me?"

It is one of the illusions most people have—that there is such a thing as inward comfort; that somebody else can give it to you or that you can find it for yourself. I am afraid there is no such thing. If you are seeking comfort you are bound to live in illusion, and when that illusion is broken you become sad because the comfort is taken away from you. So, to understand sorrow or to go beyond it, one must see actually what is inwardly taking place, and not cover it up. To point out all this is not cruelty, is it? It's not something ugly from which to shy away. When you see all this, very clearly, then you come out of it immediately, without a scratch, unblemished, fresh, untouched by the events of life. Death is inevitable for all of us; one cannot escape from it. We try to find every kind of explanation, cling to every kind of belief in the hope of going beyond it, but do what you will it is always there; tomorrow, or round the corner, or many years away—it is always there. One has to come into touch with this enormous fact of life.

"But . . ." said the uncle, and out came the traditional belief in Atman, the soul, the permanent entity which continues. He was on his own ground now, well-trodden with cunning arguments and quotations. You saw him suddenly sit up straight and the light of battle, the battle of words, came into his eyes. Sympathy, love and understanding were gone. He was on his sacred ground of belief, of tradition, trodden down by the heavy weight of conditioning: "But the Atman is in every one of us! It is reborn and continues until it realises that it is Brahman. We must go through sorrow to come to that reality. We live in illusion; the world is an illusion. There is only one reality."

And he was off! She looked at me, not paying much attention to him, and a gentle smile began to appear on her face; and we both looked at the dove which had come back, and the bright red bougainvilia.

There is nothing permanent either on earth or in ourselves. Thought can give continuity to something it thinks about; it can give permanency to a word, to an idea, to a tradition. Thought thinks itself permanent, but is it permanent? Thought is the response of memory, and is that memory permanent? It can build an image and give to that image a continuity, a permanency, calling it Atman or whatever you like, and it can remember the face of the husband or the wife and hold on to it. All this is the activity of thought which creates fear, and out of this fear there is the drive for permanency—the fear of not having a meal tomorrow, or shelter —the fear of death. This fear is the result of thought, and Brahman is the product of thought, too.

The uncle said: "Memory and thought are like a candle. You put it out and re-light it again; you forget, and you remember again later on. You die and are re-born again into another life. The flame of the candle is the same—and not the same. So in the flame there is a certain quality of continuity."

But the flame which has been put out is not the same flame as the new. There is an ending of the old for the new to be. If there is a constant modified continuity, then there is no new thing at all. The thousand yesterdays cannot be made new; even a candle burns itself out. Everything must end for the new to be.

The uncle now cannot rely on quotations or beliefs or on the sayings of others, so he withdraws into himself and becomes quiet, puzzled and rather angry, for he has been exposed to himself, and, like his niece, doesn't want to face the fact.

"I am not concerned about all this," she said. "I am utterly miserable. I have lost my husband and my son, and there are these two children left. What am I to do?"

If you are concerned about the two children, you can't be concerned about yourself and your misery. You have to look after them, educate them rightly, bring them up without the usual mediocrity. But if you are consumed by your own self-pity, which you call "the love for your husband", and if you withdraw into isolation, then you are also destroying the other two children. Consciously or unconsciously we are all utterly selfish, and so long as we get what we want we consider everything is all right. But the moment an event takes place to shatter all this, we cry out in despair, hoping to find other comforts which, of course, will again be shattered. So this process goes on, and if you want to be caught in it, knowing full well all the implications of it, then go ahead. But if you see the absurdity of it all, then you will naturally stop crying, stop isolating yourself, and live with the children with a new light and with a smile on your face.

5

Silence has many qualities. There is the silence between two noises, the silence between two notes and the widening silence in the interval between two thoughts. There is that peculiar, quiet, pervading silence that comes of an evening in the country; there is the silence through which you hear the bark of a dog in the distance or the whistle of a train as it comes up a steep grade; the silence in a house when everybody has gone to sleep, and its peculiar emphasis when you wake up in the middle of the night and listen to an owl hooting in the valley; and there is that silence before the owl's mate answers. There is the silence of an old deserted house, and the silence of a mountain; the silence between two human beings when they have seen the same thing, felt the same thing, and acted.

That night, particularly in that distant valley with the most ancient hills with their peculiar shaped boulders, the silence was as real as the wall you touched. And you looked out of the window at the brilliant stars. It was not a self-generated silence; it was not that the earth was quiet and the villagers were asleep, but it came from everywhere—from the distant stars, from those dark hills and from your own mind and heart. This silence seemed to cover everything from the tiniest grain of sand in the river-bed—which only knew running water when it rained—to the tall, spreading banyan tree and a slight breeze that was now beginning. There is the silence of the mind which is never touched by any noise, by any thought or by the passing wind of experience. It is this silence that is innocent, and so endless. When there is this silence of the mind action springs from it, and this action does not cause confusion or misery.

The meditation of a mind that is utterly silent is the benediction that man is ever seeking. In this silence every quality of silence is.

There is that strange silence that exists in a temple or in an empty church deep in the country, without the noise of tourists and worshippers; and the heavy silence that lies on water is part of that which is outside the silence of the mind.

The meditative mind contains all these varieties, changes and movements of silence. This silence of the mind is the true religious mind, and the silence of the gods is the silence of the earth. The meditative mind flows in this silence, and love is the way of this mind. In this silence there is bliss and laughter.

The uncle came back again, this time without the niece

who had lost her husband. He was a little more carefully dressed, also more disturbed and concerned, and his face had become darker because of his seriousness and anxiety. The floor on which we were sitting was hard, and the red bougainvilia was there, looking at us through the window. And the dove would probably come a little later. It always came about this time of the morning. It always sat on that branch in the same place, its back to the window and its head pointing south, and the cooing would come softly through the window.

"I would like to talk about immortality and the perfection of life as it evolves towards the ultimate reality. From what you said the other day, you have direct perception of what is true, and we, not knowing, only believe. We really don't know anything about the Atman at all; we are familiar only with the word. The symbol, for us, has become the real, and if you describe the symbol—which you did the other day —we get frightened. But in spite of this fear we cling to it, because we actually know nothing except what we've been taught, what the previous teachers have said, and the weight of tradition is always with us. So, first of all, I'd like to know for myself if there is this Reality which is permanent, this Reality, call it by whatever name you like—Atman or soul— which continues after death. I'm not frightened of death. I've faced the death of my wife and several of my children, but I am concerned about this Atman as a reality. Is there this permanent entity in me?"

When we speak of permanency we mean, don't we, something that continues in spite of the constant change around it, in spite of the experiences, in spite of all the anxieties, sorrows and brutalities? Something that is imperishable? First of all, how can one find out? Can it be sought out by thought, by words? Can you find the permanent through the impermanent? Can you find that which is changeless through that which is constantly changing—thought? Thought can give permanency to an idea, Atman or soul, and say, "This is the real", because thought breeds fear of this constant change, and out of this fear it seeks something permanent—a permanent relationship between human beings, a permanency in love. Thought itself *is* impermanent, *is* changing, so anything that it invents as permanent is, like itself, non-permanent. It can cling to a memory throughout life and call that memory permanent, and then want to know whether it will continue after death. Thought has created this thing, given it continuity, nourished it day after day and held on to it. This is the greatest illusion because thought lives in time, and what it has experienced yesterday it remembers through today and tomorrow; time is born out of this. So there is the permanency of time and the permanency which thought has given to an idea of ultimately attaining the truth. All this is the product of thought—the fear, time and achievement, the everlasting becoming.

"But who is the thinker—this thinker who has all these thoughts?"

Is there a thinker at all, or only thought which puts together the thinker? And having established him, then invents the permanent, the soul, the Atman.

"Do you mean to say that I cease to exist when I don't think?"

Has it ever happened to you, naturally, to find yourself in a state where thought is totally absent? In that state are you conscious of yourself as the thinker, the observer, the experiencer? Thought is the response of memory, and the bundle of memories is the thinker. When there is no thought is there the "me" at all, about whom we make so much fuss and noise? We are not talking of a person in amnesia, or of one who is day-dreaming or controlling thought to silence it, but of a mind that is fully awake, fully alert. If there is no thought and no word, isn't the mind in a different dimension altogether?

"Certainly there is something quite different when the self is not acting, is not asserting itself, but this need not mean that the self does not exist—just because it does not act."

Of course it exists! The "me", the ego, the bundle of memories exists. We see it existing only when it responds to a challenge, but it's there, perhaps dormant or in abeyance, waiting for the next chance to respond. A greedy man is occupied most of the time with his greed; he may have moments when it is not active, but it is always there.

"What is that living entity which expresses itself in greed?"

It is still greed. The two are not separate.

"I understand perfectly what you call the ego, the 'me', its memory, its greed, its assertiveness, its demands of all kinds, but is there nothing else except this ego? In the absence of this ego do you mean to say there is oblivion?"

When the noise of those crows stops there is something: this something is the chatter of the mind—the problems, worries, conflicts, even this enquiry into what remains after death. This question can be answered only when the mind is no longer greedy or envious. Our concern is not with what there is after the ego ceases but rather with the ending of all the attributes of the ego. That is really the problem—not what reality is, or if there is something permanent, eternal—but whether the mind, which is so conditioned by the culture in which it lives and for which it is responsible—whether such a mind can free itself and discover.

"Then how am I to begin to free myself?"

You can't free yourself. You are the seed of this misery, and when you ask "how" you are asking for a method which will destroy the "you", but in the process of destroying the "you" you are creating another "you".

"If I may ask another question, what then is immortality? Mortality is death, mortality is the way of life with its sorrow and pain. Man has searched everlastingly for an immortality, a deathless state."

Again, sir, you have come back to the question of something that is timeless, which is beyond thought. What is beyond thought is innocence, and thought, do what it will, can never touch it, for thought is always old. It is innocency, like love, that is deathless, but for that to exist the mind must be free of the thousand yesterdays with their memories. And freedom is a state in which there is no hate, no violence, no brutality. Without putting away all these things how can we ask what immortality is, what love is, what truth is?

6

If you set out to meditate it will not be meditation. If you set out to be good, goodness will never flower. If you cultivate humility, it ceases to be. Meditation is like the breeze that comes in when you leave the window open; but if you deliberately keep it open, deliberately invite it to come, it will never appear.

Meditation is not the way of thought, for thought is cunning, with infinite possibilities of self-deception, and so it will miss the way of meditation. Like love, it cannot be pursued.

The river that morning was very still. You could see on it the reflections of the clouds, of the new winter wheat and the wood beyond. Even the fisherman's boat didn't seem to disturb it. The quietness of the morning lay on the land. The sun was just coming up over the tops of the trees, and a distant voice was calling, and nearby a chanting of Sanskrit was in the air.

The parrots and the mynahs had not yet begun their search for food; the vultures, bare-necked, heavy, sat on the top of the tree waiting for the carrion to come floating down the river. Often you would see some dead animal floating by and a vulture or two would be on it, and the crows would flutter around it hoping for a bite. A dog would swim out to it, and not gaining a foothold would return to the shore and wander off. A train would pass by, making a steely clatter across the bridge, which was quite long. And beyond it, up the river, lay the city.

It was a morning full of quiet delight. Poverty, disease and pain were not yet walking on the road. There was a tottering bridge across the little stream; and where this little stream—dirty-brown—joined the big river, there it was supposed to be most holy, and there people came on festive days to bathe, men, women and children. It was cold, but they did not seem to mind. And the temple priest across the way made a lot of money; and the ugliness began.

He was a bearded man and wore a turban. He was in some kind of business and from the look of him he seemed to be prosperous, well-fed. He was slow in his walk and in his thinking. His reactions were still slower. He took several minutes to understand a simple statement. He said he had a guru of his own and, as he was passing by, he felt the urge to come up and talk about things that seemed to him important.

"Why is it," he asked, "that you are against gurus? It seems so absurd. They know, and I don't know. They can guide me, help me, tell me what to do, and save me a lot of trouble and pain. They are like a light in the darkness, and one must be guided by them otherwise one is lost, confused and in great misery. They told me that I shouldn't come and see you, for they taught me the danger of those who do not accept the traditional knowledge. They said if I listened to others I would be destroying the house they had so carefully built. But the temptation to come and see you was too strong, so here I am!"

He looked rather pleased at having yielded to temptation.

What is the need of a guru? Does he know more than you do? And what does he know? If he says that he knows, he really doesn't know, and, besides, the word is not the actual state. Can anyone teach you that extraordinary state of mind? They may be able to describe it to you, awaken your interest, your desire to possess it, experience it—but they cannot give it to you. You have to walk by yourself, you have to take the journey alone, and on that journey you have to be your own teacher and pupil.

"But all this is very difficult, isn't it?" he said, "and the steps can be made easier by those who have experienced that reality."

They become the authority and all you have to do, according to them, is just to follow, to imitate, obey, accept the image, the system which they offer. In this way you lose all initiative, all direct perception. You are merely following what they think is the way to the truth. But, unfortunately, truth has no way to it.

"What do you mean?" he cried, quite shocked.

Human beings are conditioned by propaganda, by the society in which they have been brought up—each religion asserting that its own path is the best. And there are a thousand gurus who maintain that their method, their system, their way of meditation, is the only path that leads to truth. And, if you observe, each disciple tolerates, condescendingly, the disciples of other gurus. Tolerance is the civilised acceptance of a division between people—politically, religiously and socially. Man has invented many paths, giving comfort to each believer, and so the world is broken up.

"Do you mean to say that I must give up my guru? Abandon all he has taught me? I should be lost!"

But mustn't you be lost to discover? We are afraid to be lost, to be uncertain, and so we run after those who promise heaven in the religious, political or social fields. So they really encourage fear, and hold us prisoners in that fear.

"But can I walk by myself?" he asked in an incredulous voice.

There have been so many saviours, masters, gurus, political leaders and philosophers, and not one of them has saved you from your own misery and conflict. So why follow them? Perhaps there may be quite another approach to all our problems.

"But am I serious enough to grapple with all this on my own?"

You are serious only when you begin to understand—not through somebody else—the pleasures that you are pursuing now. You are living at the level of pleasure. Not that there must not be pleasure, but if this pursuit of pleasure is the whole beginning and end of your life, then obviously you can't be serious.

"You make me feel helpless and hopeless."

You feel hopeless because you want both. You want to be serious and you want also all the pleasures the world can give. These pleasures are so small and petty, anyway, that you desire in addition the pleasure which you call "God". When you see all this for yourself, not according to somebody else, then the seeing of it makes you the disciple and the master. This is the main point. Then you are the teacher, and the taught, and the teaching.

"But," he asserted, "you are a guru. You have taught me something this morning, and I accept you as my guru."

Nothing has been taught, but you have *looked*. The looking has shown you. The looking is your guru, if you like to put it that way. But it is for you either to look or not to look. Nobody can force you. But if you look because you want to be rewarded or fear to be punished, this motive prevents the looking. To see, you must be free from all authority, tradition, fear, and thought with its cunning words. Truth is not in some far distant place; it is in the looking at what is. To see oneself as one is—in that awareness into which choice does not enter—is the beginning and end of all search.

7

Thought cannot conceive or formulate to itself the nature of space. Whatever it formulates has within it the limitation of its own boundaries. This is not the space which meditation comes upon. Thought has always a horizon. The meditative mind has no horizon. The mind cannot go from the limited to the immense, nor can it transform the limited into the limitless. The one has to cease for the other to be. Meditation is opening the door into spaciousness which cannot be imagined or speculated upon. Thought is the centre round which there is the space of idea, and this space can be expanded by further ideas. But such expansion through stimulation in any form is not the spaciousness in which there is no centre. Meditation is the understanding of this centre and so going beyond it. Silence and spaciousness go together. The immensity of silence is the immensity of the mind in which a centre does not exist. The perception of this space and silence is not of thought. Thought can perceive only its own projection, and the recognition of it is its own frontier.

You crossed the little stream over a rickety bridge of bamboo and mud. The stream joined the big river and disappeared into the waters of the strong current. The little bridge had holes in it and you had to walk rather carefully. You went up the sandy slope and passed the small temple and, a little further on, a well which was as old as the wells of the earth. It was at the corner of a village where there were many goats and hungry men and women wrapped around in dirty clothes, for it was quite cold. They fished in the big river, but somehow they were still very thin, emaciated, already old, some very crippled. In the village were weavers producing the most beautiful brocade and silk saris in dark dingy little rooms with small windows. It was a trade handed down from father to son, and middlemen and shopkeepers made the money.

You didn't go through the village but turned off to the left and followed a path which had become holy, for it was supposed that upon this path the Buddha had walked some 2,500 years ago, and pilgrims came from all over the country to walk on it. This path led through green fields, among mango groves, guava trees and through scattered temples. There was an ancient village, probably older than the Buddha, and many shrines and places where the pilgrims could spend the night. It had all become dilapidated; nobody seemed to care; the goats wandered about the place. There were large trees; one old tamarind, with vultures on top and a flock of parrots. You saw them coming in and disappearing into the green tree; they became the same colour as the leaves; you heard their screech but you could not see them.

On either side of the path stretched fields of winter wheat; and in the distance were villagers and the smoke of the fires over which they cooked. It was very still, the smoke going straight up. A bull, heavy, fierce-looking, but quite harmless, wandered through the fields, eating the grain as it was driven across the field by the farmer. It had rained during the night and the heavy dust was laid low. The sun would be hot during the day but now there were heavy clouds and it was pleasant to walk even in day-time, to smell the clean earth, to see the beauty of the land. It was a very old land, full of enchantment and human sorrow, with its poverty and those useless temples.

"You have talked a great deal about beauty and love, and after listening to you I see I don't know either what beauty is or what love is. I am an ordinary man, but I have read a great deal, both philosophy and literature. The explanations which they offer seem to be different from what you are saying. I could quote to you what the ancients of this country have said about love and beauty, and also how they have expressed it in the West, but I know you don't like quotations for they smack of authority. But, sir, if you are so inclined, we could go into this matter, and then perhaps I shall be able to understand what beauty and love may mean?"

Why is it that in our lives there is so little beauty? Why are museums with their pictures and statues necessary? Why do you have to listen to music? Or read descriptions of scenery? Good taste can be taught, or perhaps one has it naturally, but good taste is not beauty. Is it in the thing that has been put together—the sleek modern aeroplane, the compact tape-recorder, the modern hotel or the Greek temple—the beauty of line, of the very complex machine, or the curve of a beautiful bridge across a deep cavern?

"But do you mean that there is no beauty in things that are beautifully made and function perfectly? No beauty in superlative artistry?"

Of course there is. When you look at the inside of a watch it is really remarkably delicate and there is a certain quality of beauty in it, and in the ancient pillars of marble, or in the words of a poet. But if that is all beauty is, then it is only the superficial response of the senses. When you see a palm tree, single against the setting sun, is it the colour, the stillness of the palm, the quietness of the evening that make you feel the beautiful, or is beauty, like love, something that lies beyond the touch and the sight? Is it a matter of education, conditioning, that says: "This is beautiful and that is not"? Is it a matter of custom and habit and style that says: "This is squalor, but that is order and the flowering of the good"? If it is all a matter of conditioning then it is the product of culture and tradition, and therefore not beauty. If beauty is the outcome or the essence of experience, then to the man from the West and from the East, beauty is dependent upon education and tradition. Is love, like beauty, of the East or of the West, of Christianity or Hinduism, or the monopoly of the State or of an ideology? Obviously it is not any of this.

"Then what is it?"

You know, sir, austerity in self-abandonment is beauty. Without austerity there is no love, and without self-abandonment beauty has no reality. We mean by austerity not the harsh discipline of the saint or of the monk or of the commissar with their proud self-denial, or the discipline which gives them power and recognition—that is not austerity. Austerity is not harsh, not a disciplined assertion of self-importance. It is not the denial of comfort, or vows of poverty, or celibacy. Austerity is the summation of intelligence. This austerity can be only when there is self-abandonment, and it cannot be through will, through choice, through deliberate intent. It is the act of beauty that abandons, and it is love that brings the deep inward clarity of austerity. Beauty is this love, in which measurement has come to an end. Then this love, do what it will, is beauty.

"What do you mean, do what it will? If there is self-abandonment then there is nothing left for one to do."

The doing is not separate from what is. It is the separation

that brings conflict and ugliness. When there is not this
separation then living itself is the act of love. The deep inward simplicity of austerity makes for a life that has no
duality. This is the journey the mind had to take to come
upon this beauty without the word. This journey is meditation.

8

Meditation is hard work. It demands the highest form of
discipline—not conformity, not imitation, not obedience, but
a discipline which comes through constant awareness, not
only of the things about you outwardly, but also inwardly.
So meditation is not an activity of isolation but action in
everyday life which demands co-operation, sensitivity and
intelligence. Without laying the foundation of a righteous
life, meditation becomes an escape and therefore has no value
whatsoever. A righteous life is not the following of social
morality, but the freedom from envy, greed and the search
for power—which all breed enmity. The freedom from these
does not come through the activity of will but through being
aware of them through self-knowing. Without knowing the
activities of the self, meditation becomes sensuous excitement
and therefore of very little significance.

At that latitude there is hardly any twilight or dawn, and
that morning the river, wide and deep, was of molten lead.
The sun was not yet over the land but there was a lightening
in the east. The birds had not yet begun to sing their daily
chorus of the morning and the villagers were not yet calling
out to each other. The morning star was quite high in the
sky, and as you watched, it grew palèr and paler until the
sun was just over the trees and the river became silver and
gold.

Then the birds began, and the village woke up. Just then, suddenly, there appeared on the window-sill a large monkey, grey, with a black face and bushy hair over the forehead. His hands were black and his long tail hung over the window-sill into the room. He sat there very quiet, almost motionless, looking at us without a movement. We were quite close, a few feet separated us. And suddenly he stretched out his arm, and we held hands for some time. His hand was rough, black and dusty for he had climbed over the roof, over the little parapet above the window and had come down and sat there. He was quite relaxed, and what was surprising was that he was extraordinarily cheerful. There was no fear, no uneasiness; it was as though he was at home. There he was, with the river bright golden now, and beyond it the green bank and the distant trees. We must have held hands for quite a time; then, almost casually, he withdrew his hand but still remained where he was. We were looking at each other, and you could see his black eyes shining, small and full of strange curiosity. He wanted to come into the room but hesitated, then stretched his arms and his legs, reached for the parapet, and was over the roof and gone. In the evening he was there again on a tree, high up, eating something. We waved to him but there was no response.

The man he was a sannyasi, a monk, with rather a nice delicate face and sensitive hands. He was clean, and his robes had been recently washed though not ironed. He said he had come from Rishikesh where he had spent many years under a guru who had now withdrawn into the higher mountains and remained alone. He said he had been to many ashrams. He had left home many years ago, perhaps when he was twenty. He couldn't remember very well at what age he had left. He said he had parents and several sisters and brothers but he had lost touch with them completely. He had come all this way because he had heard from several gurus that he should see us, and also he had read little bits here and there. And recently he had talked to a fellow sannyasi, and so he was here. One couldn't guess his age; he was more than middle-aged, but his voice and his eyes were still young.

"It has been my lot to wander over India visiting the various centres with their gurus, some of whom are scholarly, others ignorant though with a quality which indicates that they have something in them; yet others are mere exploiters giving out mantras; these have often been abroad and become popular. There are very few who have been above all this, but among those few was my recent guru. Now he has withdrawn into a remote and isolated part of the Himalayas. A whole group of us go to see him once a year to receive his blessing."

Is isolation from the world necessary?

"Obviously one must renounce the world, for the world isn't real, and one must have a guru to teach one, for the guru has experienced reality and he will help those who follow him to realise that reality. He knows, and we don't. We are surprised that you say that no guru is necessary, for you are going against tradition. You yourself have become a guru to many, and truth is not to be found alone. One must have help—the rituals, the guidance of those who know. Perhaps ultimately one may have to stand alone, but not now. We are children and we need those who have advanced along the path. It is only by sitting at the feet of one who knows that one learns. But you seem to deny all this, and I have come to find out seriously why."

Do look at that river—the morning light on it, and those sparkling, green luscious wheatfields, and the trees beyond. There is great beauty; and the eyes that see it must be full of love to comprehend it. And to hear the rattling of that train over the iron bridge is as important as to hear the voice

of the bird. So do look—and listen to those pigeons cooing.
And look at that tamarind tree with those two green parrots.
For the eyes to see them there must be a communion with
them—with the river, with that boat passing by filled with
villagers, singing as they row. This is part of the world. If
you renounce it you are renouncing beauty and love—the
very earth itself. What you are renouncing is the society of
men, but not the things which man had made out of the
world. You are not renouncing the culture, the tradition, the
knowledge—all of that goes with you when you withdraw
from the world. You are renouncing beauty and love because
you are frightened of those two words and what lies behind
those words. Beauty is associated with sensuous reality, with
its sexual implications and the love that is involved in it. This
renunciation has made the so-called religious people self-
centred—at a higher level perhaps than with the man of
the world, but it is still self-centredness. When you have no
beauty and love there is no possibility of coming upon that
immeasurable thing. If you observe, right through the
domain of the sannyasis and the saints, this beauty and love
are far from them. They may talk about it, but they are
harsh disciplinarians, violent in their controls and demands.
So essentially, though they may put on the saffron robe or the
black robe, or the scarlet of the cardinal, they are all very
worldly. It is a profession like any other profession; certainly
it is not what is called spiritual. Some of them should be
business men and not put on airs of spirituality.

"But you know, sir, you are being rather harsh, aren't
you?"

No, we are merely stating a fact, and the fact is neither
harsh, pleasant nor unpleasant; it is so. Most of us object to
facing things as they are. But all this is fairly obvious and
quite open. Isolation is the way of life, the way of the world.
Each human being, through his self-centred activities, is

isolating himself, whether he is married or not, whether he talks of co-operation, or of nationality, achievement and success. Only when this isolation becomes extreme is there a neurosis which sometimes produces—if one has talent—art, good literature, and so on. This withdrawal from the world with all its noise, brutality, hate and pleasure is a part of the isolating process, isn't it? Only the sannyasi does it in the name of religion, or God, and the competitive man accepts it as a part of the social structure.

In this isolation you do achieve certain powers, a certain quality of austerity and abstemiousness, which give a sense of power. And power, whether of the Olympic champion, or of the Prime Minister, or of the Head of the churches and temples, is the same. Power in any form is evil—if one may use that word—and the man of power can never open the door to reality. So isolation is not the way.

Co-operation is necessary in order to live at all; and there is no co-operation with the follower or with the guru. The guru destroys the disciple and the disciple destroys the guru. In this relationship of the teacher and the taught how can there be co-operation, the working together, the enquiring together, taking the journey together? This hierarchical division which is part of the social structure, whether it be in the religious field or in the army or the business world, is essentially worldly. And when one renounces the world one is caught in worldliness.

Unworldliness is not the loin-cloth or one meal a day or repeating some meaningless though stimulating mantra or phrase. It is worldliness when you give up the world and are inwardly part of that world of envy, greed, fear, of accepting authority and the division between the one who knows and the one who doesn't know. It is still worldliness when you seek achievement, whether it be fame or the achievement of what one may call the ideal, or God, or what you will. It is

the accepted tradition of the culture that is essentially
worldly, and withdrawing into a mountain far from man
does not absolve this worldliness. Reality, under no circum-
stances, lies in that direction.

One must be alone, but this aloneness is not isolation.
This aloneness implies freedom from the world of greed, hate
and violence with all its subtle ways, and from aching loneliness and despair.

To be alone is to be an outsider who does not belong to
any religion or nation, to any belief or dogma. It is this aloneness that comes upon an innocency that has never been
touched by the mischief of man. It is innocency that can live
in the world, with all its turmoil, and yet not be of it. It is
not clothed in any particular garb. The flowering of goodness does not lie along any path, for there is no path to
truth.

9

Do not think that meditation is a continuance and an expansion of experience. In experience there is always the witness
and he is ever tied to the past. Meditation, on the contrary, is
that complete inaction which is the ending of all experience.
The action of experience has its roots in the past and so it is
time-binding; it leads to action which is inaction, and brings
disorder. Meditation is the total inaction which comes out of
a mind that sees what is, without the entanglement of the
past. This action is not a response to any challenge but is the
action of the challenge itself, in which there is no duality.
Meditation is the emptying of experience and is going on all
the time, consciously or unconsciously, so it is not an action
limited to a certain period during the day. It is a continuous
action from morning till night—the watching without the

watcher. Therefore there is no division between the daily life and meditation, the religious life and the secular life. The division comes only when the watcher is tied to time. In this division there is disarray, misery and confusion, which is the state of society.

So meditation is not individualistic, nor is it social; it transcends both and so includes both. This is love : the flowering of love is meditation.

It was cool in the morning but as the day wore on it began to be quite hot and as you went through the town along the narrow street, over-crowded, dusty, dirty, noisy, you realised that every street was like that. You almost saw the exploding of the population. The car had to go very slowly, for the people were walking right in the middle of the street. It was getting hotter now. Gradually, with a great many hootings, you got out of the town and were glad of it. You drove past the factories, and at last you were in the country.

The country was dry. It had rained some time ago and the trees were now waiting for the next rains—and they would wait for a long time. You went past villagers, cattle, bullock-carts and buffaloes which refused to move out of the middle of the road; and you went past an old temple which had an air of neglect but had the quality of an ancient sanctuary. A peacock came out of the wood; its brilliant blue neck sparkled in the sun. It didn't seem to mind the car, for it walked across the road with great dignity and disappeared in the fields.

Then you began to climb steep hills, sometimes with deep ravines on both sides. Now it was getting cooler, the trees were fresher. After winding for some time through the hills, you came to the house. By then it was quite dark. The stars became very clear. You felt you could almost reach out and touch them. The silence of the night was spreading over the land. Here man could be alone, undisturbed, and look at the stars and at himself endlessly.

The man said a tiger had killed a buffalo the day before and would surely come back to it, and would we all, later in the evening, like to see the tiger? We said we would be delighted. He replied. "Then I will go and prepare a shelter in a tree near the carcase and tie a live goat to the tree. The tiger will first come to the live goat before going back to the old kill." We replied that we would rather not see the tiger at the expense of the goat. Presently, after some talk, he left. That evening our friend said, "Let us get into the car and go into the forest, and perhaps we may come upon that tiger". So towards sunset we drove through the forest for five or six miles and of course there was no tiger. Then we returned, with the headlights lighting the road. We had given up all hope of seeing the tiger and drove on without thinking about it. Just as we turned a corner—there it was, in the middle of the road, huge, its eyes bright and fixed. The car stopped, and the animal, large and threatening, came towards us, growling. It was quite close to us now, just in front of the radiator. Then it turned and came alongside the car. We put out our hand to touch it as it went by, but the friend grabbed the arm and pulled it back sharply, for he knew something of tigers. It was of great length, and as the windows were open you could smell it and its smell was not repulsive. There was a dynamic savagery about it, and great power and beauty. Still growling it went off into the woods and we went on our way, back to the house.

He had come with his family—his wife and several children—and seemed not too prosperous, though they were fairly well clothed and well fed. The children sat silently for some time until it was suggested that they should go out and play, then they jumped up eagerly and ran out of the door. The father was some kind of official; it was a job that he had to do, and that was all. He asked: "What is happiness, and why is it that it can't continue throughout one's life? I have had moments of great happiness and also, of course, great sorrow. I have struggled to live with happiness, but there is always the sorrow. Is it possible to remain with happiness?"

What is happiness? Do you know when you are happy, or only a moment later when it is over? Is happiness pleasure, and can pleasure be constant?

"I should think, sir, at least for me, that pleasure is part of the happiness I have known. I cannot imagine happiness without pleasure. Pleasure is a primary instinct in man, and if you take it away how can there be happiness?"

We are, are we not, enquiring into this question of happiness? And if you assume anything, or have opinion or judgment in this enquiry, you will not be able to go very far. To enquire into complex human problems there must be freedom from the very beginning. If you haven't got it you are like an animal tethered to a post and can move only as far as the rope will allow. That's what always happens. We have concepts, formulas, beliefs or experiences which tether us, and from those we try to examine, look around, and this naturally prevents a very deep inquiry. So, if we may suggest, don't assume or believe, but have eyes that can see very clearly. If happiness is pleasure, then it is also pain. You cannot separate pleasure from pain. Don't they always go together?

So what is pleasure and what is happiness? You know, sir, if, in examining a flower, you tear its petals away one by one, there is no flower left at all. You will have in your hands bits of the flower and the bits don't make the beauty of the flower. So in looking at this question we are not analysing intellectually, thereby making the whole thing arid, meaningless and empty. We are looking at it with eyes that care very much, with eyes that understand, with eyes that touch but do not tear. So please don't tear at it and go away empty handed. Leave the analytical mind alone.

Pleasure is encouraged by thought, isn't it? Thought can give it a continuity, the appearance of duration which we call happiness; as thought can also give a duration to sorrow. Thought says: "This I like and that I don't like. I would like to keep this and throw away that." But thought has made up both, and happiness now has become the way of thought. When you say: "I want to remain in that state of happiness"—you are the thought, you are the memory of the previous experience which you call pleasure and happiness.

So the past, or yesterday, or many yesterdays ago, which is thought, is saying: "I would like to live in that state of happiness which I have had." You are making the dead past into an actuality in the present and you are afraid of losing it tomorrow. Thus you have built a chain of continuity. This continuity has its roots in the ashes of yesterday, and therefore it is not a living thing at all. Nothing can blossom in ashes—and thought is ashes. So you have made happiness a thing of thought, and it *is* for you a thing of thought.

But is there something other than pleasure, pain, happiness and sorrow? Is there a bliss, an ecstasy, that is not touched by thought? For thought is very trivial, and there is nothing original about it. In asking this question, thought must abandon itself. When thought abandons itself there is the discipline of the abandonment, which becomes the grace of austerity. Then austerity is not harsh and brutal. Harsh austerity is the product of thought as a revulsion against pleasure and indulgence.

From this deep self-abandonment—which is thought abandoning itself, for it sees clearly its own danger—the whole structure of the mind becomes quiet. It is really a state of pure attention and out of this comes a bliss, an ecstasy, that cannot be put into words. When it is put into words it is not the real.

10

Meditation is a movement in stillness. Silence of the mind is the way of action. Action born of thought is inaction, which breeds disorder. This silence is not the product of thought, nor is it the ending of the chattering of the mind. A still mind is possible only when the brain itself is quiet. The brain cells—which have been conditioned for so long to react, to project, to defend, to assert—become quiet only through the seeing of what actually is. From this silence, action which does not bring about disorder is possible only when the observer, the centre, the experiencer, has come to an end—for then the seeing is the doing. Seeing is possible only out of a silence in which all evaluation and moral values have come to an end.

This temple was older than its gods. They remained, prisoners in the temple, but the temple itself was far more ancient. It had thick walls and pillars in the corridors, carved with horses, gods and angels. They had a certain quality of beauty, and as you passed them you wondered what would happen if they all came alive, including the innermost god.

They said that this temple, especially the innermost sanctuary, went back far beyond the imagination of time. As you wandered through the various corridors, lit by the morning sun and with sharp, clear shadows, you wondered what it was all about—how man has made gods out of his own mind and carved them with his hands and put them into temples and churches and worshipped them.

The temples of the ancient times had a strange beauty and power. They seemed to be born out of the very earth itself. This temple was almost as old as man, and the gods in it were clothed in silks, garlanded, and awakened from their sleep with chants, with incense and with bells. The incense, which had been burned for many centuries past, seemed to pervade the whole of the temple, which was vast and must have covered several acres.

People seemed to have come here from all over the country, the rich and the poor, but only a certain class were allowed inside the sanctuary itself. You entered through a low stone door, stepping over a parapet which was worn down through time. Outside the sanctuary there were guardians in stone, and when you came into it there were priests, naked down to the waist, chanting, solemn and dignified. They were all rather well fed, with big tummies and delicate hands. Their voices were hoarse, for they had been chanting for so many years; and the God, or the Goddess, was almost shapeless. There must have been a face at one time but the features had almost gone. The jewels must have been beyond price.

When the chanting stopped there was a stillness as though the very earth had stopped in its rotation. In here there was no sunshine, and the light came only from the wicks burning in the oil. Those wicks had blackened the ceiling and the place was quite mysteriously dark.

All gods must be worshipped in mystery and in darkness, otherwise they have no existence.

When you came out into the open strong light of the sun and looked at the blue sky and the tall waving palm trees you wondered why it is that man worships himself as the image which he has made with his hands and mind. Fear, and that lovely blue sky, seemed so far apart.

He was a young man, clean, sharp of face, bright-eyed, with a quick smile. We sat on the floor in a little room overlooking a small garden. The garden was full of roses, from white to almost black. A parrot was on a branch, hanging upside down, with its bright eyes and red beak. It was looking at another much smaller bird.

He spoke English fairly well, but was rather hesitant in the use of words, and for the moment he seemed serious. He asked: "What is a religious life? I have asked various gurus and they have given the standard replies, and I would like, if I may, to ask you the same question. I had a good job, but as I am not married, I gave it up because I am drawn deeply by religion and want to find out what it means to lead a religious life in a world that is so irreligious."

Instead of asking what a religious life is, wouldn't it be better, if I may suggest it, to ask what living is? Then perhaps we may understand what a truly religious life is. The so-called religious life varies from clime to clime, from sect to sect, from belief to belief; and man suffers through the propaganda of the organised vested interests of religions. If we could set aside all that—not only the beliefs, the dogmas and rituals but also the respectability which is entailed in the culture of religion—then perhaps we could find out what a religious life is untouched by the thought of man.

But before we do that, let us, as we said, find out what living is. The actuality of living is the daily grind, the routine, with its struggle and conflict; it is the ache of loneliness, the misery and the squalor of poverty and riches, the ambition, the search for fulfilment, the success and the sorrow—these cover the whole field of our life. This is what we call living—

gaining and losing a battle, and the endless pursuit of pleasure.

In contrast to this, or in opposition to this, there is what is called religious living or a spiritual life. But the opposite contains the very seed of its own opposite and so, though it may appear different, actually it is not. You may change the outer garment but the inner essence of what was and of what must be is the same. This duality is the product of thought and so it breeds more conflict; and the corridor of this conflict is endless. All this we know—we have been told it by others or we have felt it for ourselves and all this we call living.

The religious life is not on the other side of the river, it is on this side—the side of the whole travail of man. It is this that we have to understand, and the action of understanding is the religious act—not putting on ashes, wearing a loin cloth or a mitre, sitting in the seat of the mighty or being carried on an elephant.

The seeing of the whole condition, the pleasure and the misery of man, is of the first importance—not the speculation as to what a religious life should be. What should be is a myth; it is the morality which thought and fancy have put together, and one must deny this morality—the social, the religious and the industrial. This denial is not of the intellect but is an actual slipping out of the pattern of that morality which is immoral.

So the question really is: Is it possible to step out of this pattern? It is thought which has created this frightening mess and misery, and which has prevented both religion and the religious life. Thought thinks that it can step out of the pattern, but if it does it will still be an act of thought, for thought has no reality and therefore it will create another illusion.

Going beyond this pattern is not an act of thought. This

must be clearly understood, otherwise you will be caught again in the prison of thought. After all, the "you" is a bundle of memory, tradition and the knowledge of a thousand yesterdays. So only with the ending of sorrow, for sorrow is the result of thought, can you step out of the world of war, hate, envy and violence. This act of stepping out is the religious life. This religious life has no belief whatsoever, for it has no tomorrow.

"Aren't you asking, sir, for an impossible thing? Aren't you asking for a miracle? How can I step out of it all without thought? Thought is my very being!"

That's just it! This very being, which is thought, has to come to an end. This very self-centredness with its activities must naturally and easily die. It is in this death alone that there is the beginning of the new religious life.

II

If you deliberately take an attitude, a posture, in order to meditate, then it becomes a plaything, a toy of the mind. If you determine to extricate yourself from the confusion and the misery of life, then it becomes an experience of imagination—and this is not meditation. The conscious mind or the unconscious mind must have no part in it; they must not even be aware of the extent and beauty of meditation—if they are, then you might just as well go and buy a romantic novel.

In the total attention of meditation there is no knowing, no recognition, nor the remembrance of something that has happened. Time and thought have entirely come to an end, for they are the centre which limits its own vision.

At the moment of light, thought withers away, and the conscious effort to experience and the remembrance of it, is the word that has been. And the word is never the actual. At that moment—which is not of time—the ultimate is the immediate, but that ultimate has no symbol, is of no person, of no god.

That morning, especially so early, the valley was extraordinarily quiet. The owl had stopped hooting and there was no reply from its mate over in the distant hills. No dog was barking and the village was not yet awake. In the east there was a glow, a promise, and the Southern Cross had not yet faded. There was not even a whisper among the leaves, and the earth itself seemed to have stopped in its rotation. You could feel the silence, touch it, smell it, and it had that quality of penetration. It wasn't the silence outside in those hills, among the trees, that was still; you were of it. You and it were not two separate things. The division between noise and silence had no meaning. And those hills, dark, without a movement, were of it, as you were.

This silence was very active. It was not the negation of noise, and strangely that morning it had come through the window like some perfume, and with it came a sense, a feeling, of the absolute. As you looked out of the window, the distance between all things disappeared, and your eyes opened with the dawn and saw everything anew.

"I am interested in sex, social equality, and God. These are the only things that matter in life, and nothing else. Politics, religions with their priests and promises, with their rituals and confessions, seem so insulting. They really don't answer a thing, they have never really solved any problems, they have helped only to postpone them. They've condemned sex, in different ways, and they have sustained social inequalities, and the god of their mind is a stone which they have clothed with love and its sentiment. Personally I have no use for it at all. I only tell you this so that we can put all that aside and concern ourselves with these three issues—sex, social misery, and that thing called God.

"To me, sex is necessary as food is necessary. Nature has made man and woman and the enjoyment of the night. To me that is as important as the discovery of that truth which may be called God. And it is as important to feel for your neighbour as to have love for the woman of your house. Sex is not a problem. I enjoy it, but there is in me a fear of some unknown thing, and it is this fear and pain that I must understand—not as a problem to be solved but rather as something that I have to go into so that I am really cleansed of it. So I would like, if you have the time, to consider these things with you."

Can we begin with the last and not with the first, then perhaps the other issues can be more deeply understood; then perhaps they will have a different content than pleasure can give?

Do you want your belief to be strengthened or do you want actually to see reality—not experience it, but actually see it with a mind and heart that are highly attentive and clear? Belief is one thing and seeing is another. Belief leads to darkness, as faith does. It leads you to the church, to the dark temples and to the pleasurable sensations of rituals. Along that way there is no reality, there is only fancy, the imaginative furnishings that fill the church.

If you deny fear, belief is unnecessary, but if you cling to belief and dogma then fear has its way. Belief is not only according to the religious sanctions; it comes into being though you may not belong to any religion. You may have your own individualistic, exclusive belief—but it is not the light of clarity. Thought invests in belief to protect itself against fear which it has brought into being. And the way of thought is not the freedom of attention which sees truth.

The immeasurable cannot be sought by thought, for thought has always a measure. The sublime is not within the structure of thought and reason, nor is it the product of emotion and sentiment. The negation of thought is attention; as the negation of thought is love. If you are seeking the highest, you will not find it; it must come to you, if you are lucky—and luck is the open window of your heart, not of thought.

"This is rather difficult, isn't it? You are asking me to deny the whole structure of myself, the me that I have very carefully nourished and sustained. I had thought the pleasure of what may be called God to be everlasting. It is my security; in it is all my hope and delight; and now you ask me to put all that aside. Is it possible? And do I really want to? Also, aren't you promising me something as a reward if I put it all aside? Of course I see that you are not actually offering me a reward, but can I actually—not only with my lips—put aside completely the thing that I have always lived on?"

If you try to put it aside deliberately it will become a conflict, pain and endless misery. But if you see the truth of it—as you see the truth of that lamp, the flickering light, the wick and the brass stem—then you will have stepped into another dimension. In this dimension love has no social problems; there is no racial, class or intellectual division. It is only the unequal who feel the necessity for equality. It is the superior who needs to keep his division, his class, his ways. And the inferior is ever striving to become the superior; the oppressed to become the oppressor. So merely to legislate—though such legislation is necessary—does not bring about the end of division with its cruelty; nor does it end the division between labour and status. We use work to achieve status, and the whole cycle of inequality begins. The problems of society are not ended by the morality that society has invented. Love has no morality, and love is not reform. When love becomes pleasure, then pain is inevitable. Love is not thought and it is thought that gives pleasure—as sexual pleasure and as the pleasure of achievement. Thought strengthens and gives continuity to the pleasure of the moment. Thought, by thinking about that pleasure, gives it the vitality of the next moment of pleasure. This demand for pleasure is what we call sex, is it not? With it goes a great deal of affection, tenderness, care, companionship, and all the rest of it, but through it all there is the thread of pain and fear. And thought, by its activity, makes this thread unbreakable.

"But you can't remove pleasure from sex! I live by that pleasure; I like it. To me it is far more important than having money, position or prestige. I also see that pleasure brings with it pain, but the pleasure predominates over the pain, so I don't mind."

When this pleasure which you so delight in comes to an end—with age, through accident, with time—then you are caught; then sorrow is your shadow. But love is not pleasure, nor is it the product of desire, and that is why, sir, one must enter into a different dimension. In that our problems—and all issues—are resolved. Without that, do what you will, there is sorrow and confusion.

12

A great many birds were flying overhead, some crossing the wide river and others, high up in the sky, going round in wide circles with hardly a movement of the wing. Those that were high up were mostly vultures and in the bright sun they were mere specks, tacking against the breeze. They were clumsy on land with their naked necks and wide, heavy wings. There were a few of them on the tamarind tree, and the crows were teasing them. One crow, especially, was after a vulture, trying to perch on him. The vulture got bored and took to the wing, and the crow which had been harassing him came in from behind and sat on the vulture's back as it flew. It was really quite a curious sight—the vulture with the black crow on top of it. The crow seemed to be thoroughly enjoying himself and the vulture was trying to get rid of him. Eventually the crow flew off across the river and disappeared into the woods.

The parrots came across the river, zig-zagging, screeching, telling the whole world they were coming. They were bright green, with red beaks, and there were several in that tamarind tree. They would come out in the morning, go down the river and sometimes would come back screeching, but more often they remained away all day and only returned in the late afternoon, having stolen the grain from the fields and whatever fruit they could find. You saw them for a few seconds among the tamarind leaves, and then they would disappear. You couldn't really follow them among the tiny green leaves of the tree. They had a hole in the trunk and there they lived, male and female, and they seemed to be so happy, screeching their joy as they flew out. In the evening and early morning the sun made a path—golden in the morning and silver in the evening—across the river. No wonder men worship rivers; it is better than worshipping images with all the rituals and beliefs. The river was alive, deep and full, always in movement; and the little pools beside the bank were always stagnant.

Each human being isolates himself in the little pool, and there decays; he never enters into the full current of the river. Somehow that river, made so filthy by human beings higher up, was clean in the middle, blue-green and deep. It was a splendid river, especially in the early morning before the sun came up; it was so still, motionless, of the colour of molten silver. And, as the sun came up over the trees, it became golden, and then turned again into a silvery path; and the water came alive.

In that room overlooking the river it was cool, almost cold, for it was early winter. A man, sitting opposite with his wife, was young, and she was younger still. We sat on the carpet placed on a rather cold, hard floor. They weren't interested in looking at the river, and when it was pointed out to them —its width, its beauty, and the green bank on the other side —they acknowledged it with a polite gesture. They had come some distance, from the north by bus and train, and were eager to talk about the things they had in mind; the river was something they could look at later when they had time.

He said: "Man can never be free; he is tied to his family, to his children, to his job. Until he dies he has responsibilities. Unless, of course," he added, "he becomes a sannyasi, a monk."

He saw the necessity of being free, yet he felt it was something he could not achieve in this competitive, brutal world. His wife listened to him with a rather surprised look, pleased to find that her man could be serious and could express himself quite well in English. It gave her a sense of possessive pride. He was totally unaware of this as she was sitting a little behind him.

"Can one be free, ever?" he asked. "Some political writers and theorists, like the Communists, say that freedom is something bourgeois, unattainable and unreal, while the democratic world talks a great deal about freedom. So do the capitalists, and, of course, every religion preaches it and promises it, though they see to it that man is made a prisoner of their particular beliefs and ideologies—denying their promises by their acts. I've come to find out, not merely

intellectually, if man, if I, can really be free in this world.
I'm taking a holiday from my job to come here; for two
days I am free from my work—from the routine of the office
and the usual life of the little town where I live. If I had
more money I'd be freer and be able to go where I like and
do what I want to do, perhaps paint, or travel. But that is
impossible as my salary is limited and I have responsibilities;
I am a prisoner to my responsibilities." ✓

His wife couldn't make out all this but she pricked up her
ears at the word "responsibilities". She may have been
wondering whether he wanted to leave home and wander the
face of the earth.

"These responsibilities," he went on, "prevent me from
being free both outwardly and inwardly. I can understand
that man cannot be completely free from the world of the
post office, the market, the office and so on, and I'm not
seeking freedom there. What I have come to find out is if it
is at all possible to be free inwardly?"

The pigeons on the veranda were cooing, fluttering about,
and the parrots screeched across the window and the sun
shone on their bright green wings.

What is freedom? Is it an idea, or a feeling that thought
breeds because it is caught in a series of problems, anxieties,
and so on? Is freedom a result, a reward, a thing that lies
at the end of a process? Is it freedom when you free yourself
from anger? Or is it being able to do what you want to do?
Is it freedom when you find responsibility a burden and
push it aside? Is it freedom when you resist, or when you
yield? Can thought give this freedom, can any action give
it?

"I'm afraid you will have to go a little bit slower."

Is freedom the opposite of slavery? Is it freedom when,
being in a prison and knowing you are in prison and being
aware of all the restraints of the prison, you imagine freedom?

Can imagination ever give freedom or is it a fancy of thought? What we actually know, and what actually is, is bondage—not only to outward things, to the house, to the family, to the job—but also inwardly, to traditions, to habits, to the pleasure of domination and possession, to fear, to achievement and to so many other things. When success brings great pleasure one never talks about freedom from it, or thinks about it. We talk of freedom only when there is pain. We are bound to all these things, both inwardly and outwardly, and this bondage is what is. And the resistance to what is, is what we call freedom. One resists, or escapes from, or tries to suppress what is, hoping thereby to come to some form of freedom. We know inwardly only two things— bondage and resistance; and resistance creates the bondage.

"Sorry, I don't understand at all."

When you resist anger or hatred, what has actually taken place? You build a wall against hatred, but it is still there; the wall merely hides it from you. Or you determine not to be angry, but this determination is part of the anger, and the very resistance strengthens the anger. You can see it in yourself if you observe this fact. When you resist, control, suppress, or try to transcend—which are all the same thing for they are all acts of the will—you have thickened the wall of resistance, and so you become more and more enslaved, narrow, petty. And it is from this pettiness, this narrowness, that you want to be free, and that very want is the reaction which is going to create another barrier, more pettiness. So we move from one resistance, one barrier, to another—sometimes giving to the wall of resistance a different colouring, a different quality, or some word of nobility. But resistance is bondage, and bondage is pain.

"Does this mean that, outwardly, one should let anybody kick one around as they will, and that, inwardly, one's anger, etc., should be given free rein?"

It seems that you have not listened to what has been said. When it is a matter of pleasure you don't mind the kick of it, the feeling of delight; but when that kick becomes painful, then you resist. You want to be free from the pain and yet hold on to the pleasure. The holding on to the pleasure is the resistance.

It is natural to respond; if you do not respond physically to the prick of a pin it means you are numbed. Inwardly, too, if you do not respond, something is wrong. But the way in which you respond and the nature of the response is important, not the response itself. When somebody flatters you, you respond; and you respond when somebody insults you. Both are resistances—one of pleasure and the other of pain. The one you keep and the other you either disregard or wish to retaliate against. But both are resistances. Both the keeping and the rejecting are a form of resistance; and freedom is not resistance.

"Is it possible for me to respond without the resistance of either pleasure or pain?"

What do *you* think, sir? What do *you* feel? Are you putting the question to me or to yourself? If an outsider, an outside agency, answers that question for you, then you rely on it, then that reliance becomes the authority, which is a resistance. Then again you want to be free of *that* authority! So how can you ask this question of another?

"You might point it out to me, and if I then see it, authority is not involved, is it?"

But we have pointed out to you what actually *is*. See what actually is, without responding to it with pleasure or with pain. Freedom is seeing. Seeing is freedom. You can see only in freedom.

"This seeing may be an act of freedom, but what effect has it on my bondage which is the what is, which is the thing seen?"

When you say the seeing *may be* an act of freedom, it is a supposition, so your seeing is also a supposition. Then you don't actually see what is.

"I don't know sir. I see my mother-in-law bullying me; does she stop it because I see it?"

See the action of your mother-in-law, and see your responses, without the further responses of pleasure and pain. See it in freedom. Your action may then be to ignore what she says completely, or to walk out. But the walking out or the disregarding her is not a resistance. This choiceless awareness is freedom. The action from that freedom cannot be predicted, systematised, or put into the framework of social morality. This choiceless awareness is non-political, it does not belong to any "ism"; it is not the product of thought.

13

"I want to know God," he said vehemently; he almost shouted it. The vultures were on the usual tree, and the train was rattling across the bridge, and the river flowed on—here it was very wide, very quiet and very deep. Early that morning you could smell the water from a distance; high on the bank overlooking the river you could smell it—the freshness, the cleanliness of it in the morning air. The day had not yet spoilt it. The parrots were screeching across the window, going to the fields, and later they would return to the tamarind. The crows, by the dozen, were crossing the river, high in the air, and they would come down on the trees and among the fields across the river. It was a clear morning of winter, cold but bright, and there was not a cloud in the sky. As you watched the light of the early morning sun on the river, meditation was going on. The very light was part of that meditation when you looked at the bright dancing water in the quiet morning—not with a mind that was translating it into some meaning, but with eyes that saw the light and nothing else.

Light, like sound, is an extraordinary thing. There is the light that painters try to put on a canvas; there is the light that cameras capture; there is the light of a single lamp in a dark night, or the light that is on the face of another, the light that lies behind the eyes. The light that the eyes see is not the light on the water; that light is so different, so vast that it cannot enter into the narrow field of the eye. That light, like sound, moved endlessly—outward and inward— like the tide of the sea. And if you kept very still, you went with it, not in imagination or sensuously; you went with it unknowingly, without the measure of time.

The beauty of that light, like love, is not to be touched, not to be put into a word. But there it was—in the shade, in the open, in the house, on the window across the way, and in the laughter of those children. Without that light what you see is of so little importance, for the light is everything; and the light of meditation was on the water. It would be there in the evening again, during the night, and when the sun rose over the trees, making the river golden. Meditation is that light in the mind which lights the way for action; and without that light there is no love.

He was a big man, clean-shaven, and his head was shaven too. We sat on the floor in that little room overlooking the river. The floor was cold, for it was winter. He had the dignity of a man who possesses little and who is not greatly frightened of what people say.

"I want to know God. I know it's not the fashionable thing nowadays. The students, the coming generation with their revolts, with their political activities, with their reasonable and unreasonable demands, scoff at all religion. And they are quite right too, for look what the priests have done with it! Naturally the younger generation do not want anything of it. To them, what the temples and churches stand for is the exploitation of man. They distrust completely the hierarchical priestly outlook—with the saviours, the ceremonies, and all that nonsense. I agree with them. I have helped some of them to revolt against it all. But I still want to know God. I have been a Communist but I left the party long ago, for the Communists, too, have their gods, their dogmas and theoreticians. I was really a very ardent Communist, for at the beginning they promised something—a great, a real revolution. But now they have all the things the Capitalists have; they have gone the way of the world. I have dabbled in social reform and have been active in politics, but I have left all that behind because I don't see that man will ever be free of his despair and anxiety and fear through science and technology. Perhaps there's only one way. I'm not in any way superstitious and I don't think I have any fear of life. I have been through it all and, as you see, I have still many years before me. I want to know what God is. I have asked some of the wandering monks, and those who everlastingly say, God *is*, you have only to look, and those who become mysterious and offer some method. I am wary of all those traps. So here I am, for I feel I must find out."

We sat in silence for some time. The parrots were passing the window, screeching, and the light was on their bright green wings and their red beaks.

Do you think you can find out? Do you think that by seeking you will come upon it? Do you think you can experience it? Do you think that the measure of your mind is going to come upon the measureless? How are you going to find out? How will you know? How will you be able to recognise it?

"I really don't know," he replied. "But I will know when it is the real."

You mean you will know it by your mind, by your heart, by your intelligence?

"No. The knowing is not dependent on any of these. I know very well the danger of the senses. I am aware how easily illusions are created."

To know is to experience, isn't it? To experience is to recognise, and recognition is memory and association. If what you mean by "knowing" is the result of a past incident, a memory, a thing that has happened before, then it is the knowing of what *has* happened. Can you know what *is* happening, what is actually taking place? Or, can you only know it a moment afterwards, when it is over? What is actually happening is out of time; knowing is always in time. You look at the happening with the eyes of time, which names it, translates it, and records it. This is what is called knowing, both analytically and through instant recognition. Into this field of knowing you want to bring that which is on the other side of the hill, or behind that tree. And you insist that you must know, that you must experience it and hold it. Can you hold those sweeping waters in your mind or in your hand? What you hold is the word and what your eyes have seen, and this seeing put into words, and the memory of those words. But the memory is not that water—and never will be.

"All right," he said, "then how shall I come upon it? I have in my long and studious life found that nothing is going to save man—no institution, no social pattern, nothing, so I've stopped reading. But man must be saved, he must come out of this somehow, and my urgent demand to find God is the cry out of a great anxiety for man. This violence that is spreading is consuming man. I know all the arguments for and against it. Once I had hope, but now I am stripped of all hope. I am really completely at the end of my tether. I am not asking this question out of despair or to renew hope. I just can't see any light. So I have come to ask this one question : Can you help me to uncover reality—if there *is* a reality?"

Again we were silent for some time. And the cooing of pigeons came into the room.

"I see what you mean. I've never before been so utterly silent. The question is there, outside of this silence, and when I look out of this silence at the question, it recedes. So you mean that it is only in this silence, in this complete and unpremeditated silence, that there is the measureless?"

Another train was rattling across the bridge.

This invites all the foolishness and the hysteria of mysticism—a vague, inarticulate sentiment which breeds illusion. No, sir, this is not what we mean. It's hard work to put away all illusions—the political, the religious, the illusion of the future. We never discover anything for ourselves. We think we do, and that is one of the greatest illusions, which is thought. It is hard work to see clearly into this mess, into the insanity which man has woven around himself. You need a very, very sane mind to see, and to be free. These two, seeing and freedom, are absolutely necessary. Freedom from the urge to see, freedom from the hope that man always gives to science, to technology and to religious discoveries. This hope breeds illusion. To see this is freedom, and when there is freedom you do not invite. Then the mind itself has become the measureless.

14

He was an old monk, revered by many thousands. He had kept his body well, his head was shaven and he wore the usual saffron-coloured sannyasi robe. He carried a big stick which had seen many seasons, and a pair of sand-shoes, rather worn out. We sat on a bench overlooking the river, high up, with the railway bridge to our right and the river winding down round a big curve to our left. The other side of the bank, that morning, was in a heavy mist, and you could just see the tops of the trees. It was as though they were floating on the extended river. There was not a breath of air, and the swallows were flying low near the water's edge. That river was very old and sacred, and people came from very far to die on its banks and to be burnt there. It was worshipped, praised in chants and held most sacred. Every kind of filth was thrown into it; people bathed in it, drank it, washed their clothes in it; you saw people on the banks meditating, their eyes closed, sitting very straight and still. It was a river that gave abundantly, but man was polluting it. In the rainy season it would rise from twenty to thirty feet, carry away all the filth, and cover the land with silt which gave nourishment to the peasants along its bank. It came down in great curves, and sometimes you would see whole trees going by, uprooted by the strong current. You would also see dead animals, on which were perched vultures and crows, fighting with each other, and occasionally an arm or a leg or even the whole body of some human being.

That morning the river was lovely, there was not a ripple on it. The other bank seemed far away. The sun had been up for several hours and the mist had not yet gone, and the river, like some mysterious being, flowed on. The monk was very familiar with that river; he had spent many years on its banks, surrounded by his disciples, and he took it almost for granted that it would be there always, that as long as man lived it would live also. He had got used to it, and therein lay the pity of it. Now he looked at it with eyes that had seen it many thousands of times. One gets used to beauty and to ugliness, and the freshness of the day is gone.

"Why are you," he asked, in a rather authoritative voice, "against morality, against the scriptures which we hold most sacred? Probably you have been spoilt by the West where freedom is licentiousness and where they do not even know, except the few, what real discipline means. Obviously you have not read any of our sacred books. I was here the other morning when you were talking and I was rather aghast at what you were saying about the gods, the priests, the saints and the gurus. How can man live without any of these? If he does, he becomes materialistic, worldly, utterly brutal. You seem to deny all the knowledge that we hold most sacred. Why? I know you are serious. We have followed you from a distance for many years. We have watched you as a brother. We thought you belonged to us. But since you have renounced all these things we have become strangers, and it seems a thousand pities that we are walking on different paths."

What is sacred? Is the image in the temple, the symbol, the word, sacred? Where does sacredness lie? In that tree, or in that peasant-woman carrying that heavy load? You invest sacredness, don't you, in things you consider holy, worthwhile, meaningful? But what value has the image, carved by the hand or by the mind? That woman, that tree, that bird, the living things, seem to have but a passing importance for you. You divide life into that which is sacred and that which is not, that which is immoral and that which is moral. This division begets misery and violence. Either everything is sacred, or nothing is sacred. Either what you say, your words, your thoughts, your chants are serious, or they are there to beguile the mind into some kind of enchantment, which becomes illusion, and therefore not serious at all. There *is* something sacred, but it is not in the word, not in the statue or in the image that thought has built.

He looked rather puzzled and not at all sure where this was leading, so he interrupted: "We are not actually discussing what is and what is not sacred, but rather, one would like to know why you decry discipline?"

Discipline, as it is generally understood, is conformity to a pattern of silly political, social or religious sanctions. This conformity implies, doesn't it, imitation, suppression, or some form of transcendence of the actual state? In this discipline there is obviously a continuous struggle, a conflict that distorts the quality of the mind. One conforms because of a promised or hoped-for reward. One disciplines oneself in order to get something. In order to achieve something one obeys and submits, and the pattern—whether it be the Communist pattern, the religious pattern or one's own—becomes the authority. In this there is no freedom at all. Discipline means to learn; and learning denies all authority and obedience. To see all this is not an analytical process. To see the implications involved in this whole structure of discipline is itself discipline, which is to learn all about this structure. And the learning is not a matter of gathering information, but of seeing the structure and the nature of it immediately. That is true discipline, because you are learning, and not conforming. To learn there must be freedom.

"Does this imply," he asked, "that you do just what you want? That you disregard the authority of the State?"

Of course not, sir. Naturally you have to accept the law of the State or of the policeman, until such law undergoes a change. You have to drive on one side of the road, not all over the road, for there are other cars too, so one has to follow the rule of the road. If one did exactly what one liked—which we surreptitiously do anyway—there would be utter chaos; and that is exactly what there is. The businessman, the politician and almost every human being is pursuing, under cover of respectability, his own secret desires and appetites, and this is producing chaos in the world. We want to cover this up by passing laws, sanctions, and so on. This is not freedom. Throughout the world there are people who have sacred books, modern or ancient. They repeat from them, put them into song, and quote them endlessly, but in their hearts they are violent, greedy, searching for power. Do these so-called sacred books matter at all? They have no actual meaning. What matters is man's utter selfishness, his constant violence, hate and enmity—not the books, the temples, the churches, the mosques.

Under the robe the monk is frightened. He has his own appetites, he is burning with desire, and the robe is merely an escape from this fact.

In transcending these agonies of man we spend our time quarrelling about which books are most sacred than others, and this is so utterly immature.

"Then you must also deny tradition. . . . Do you?"

To carry the past over to the present, to translate the movement of the present in terms of the past, destroys the living beauty of the present. This land, and almost every land, is burdened with tradition, entrenched in high places and in the village hut. There is nothing sacred about tradition, however ancient or modern. The brain carries the memory of yesterday, which is tradition, and is frightened to let go, because it cannot face something new. Tradition becomes our security, and when the mind is secure it is in decay. One must take the journey unburdened, sweetly, without any effort, never stopping at any shrine, at any monument, or for any hero, social or religious—alone with beauty and love.

"But we monks are always alone, aren't we?" he asked. "I have renounced the world and taken a vow of poverty and chastity."

You are not alone, sir, because the very vow binds you—

as it does the man who takes the vow when he gets married. If we may point out, you are not alone because you are a Hindu, just as you would not be alone if you were a Buddhist, or a Muslim, or a Christian or a Communist. You are committed, and how can a man be alone when he is committed, when he has given himself over to some form of ideation, which brings its own activity? The word itself, "alone", means what it says—uninfluenced, innocent, free and whole, not broken up. When you are alone you may live in this world but you will always be an outsider. Only in aloneness can there be complete action and co-operation; for love is always whole.

15

That morning the river was tarnished silver, for it was cloudy and cold. The leaves were covered with dust, and everywhere there was a thin layer of it—in the room, on the veranda and on the chair. It was getting colder; it must have snowed heavily in the Himalayas; one could feel the biting wind from the north, even the birds were aware of it. But the river that morning had a strange movement of its own; it didn't seem to be ruffled by the wind, it seemed almost motionless and had that timeless quality which all waters seem to have. How beautiful it was! No wonder people have made it into a sacred river. You could sit there, on that veranda, and meditatively watch it endlessly. You weren't day-dreaming; your thoughts weren't in any direction—they were simply absent.

And as you watched the light on that river, somehow you seemed to lose yourself, and as you closed your eyes there was a penetration into a void that was full of blessing. This was bliss.

*   *   *

He came again that morning, with a young man. He was the monk who had talked about discipline, sacred books and the authority of tradition. His face was freshly washed, and so were his robes. The young man seemed rather nervous. He had come with the monk, who was probably his guru, and was waiting for him to speak first. He looked at the river but he was thinking of other things. Presently the sannyasi said :

"I have come again but this time to talk about love and sensuality. We, who have taken the vow of chastity, have our sensuous problems. The vow is only a means of resisting our uncontrollable desires. I am an old man now, and these desires no longer burn me. Before I took the vows I was married. My wife died, and I left my home and went through a period of agony, of intolerable biological urges; I fought them night and day. It was a very difficult time, full of loneliness, frustration, fears of madness, and neurotic outbursts. Even now I daren't think about it too much. And this young man has come with me because I think he is going through the same problem. He wants to give up the world and take the vow of poverty and chastity, as I did. I have been talking to him for many weeks, and I thought it might be worthwhile if we could both talk over this problem with you, this problem of sex and love. I hope you don't mind if we talk quite frankly."

If we are going to concern ourselves with this matter, first, if we may suggest it, don't start to examine from a position, or an attitude, or a principle, for this will prevent you from exploration. If you are against sex, or if you insist that it is necessary to life, that it is a part of living, any such assumption will prevent real perception. We should put away any conclusion, and so be free to look, to examine.

There were a few drops of rain now, and the birds had become quiet, for it was going to rain heavily, and the leaves once again would be fresh and green, full of light and colour.

There was a smell of rain, and the strange quietness that comes before a storm was on the land.

So we have two problems—love and sex. The one is an abstract idea, the other is an actual daily biological urge—a fact that exists and cannot be denied. Let us first find out what love is, not as an abstract idea but what it actually is. What is it? Is it merely a sensuous delight, cultivated by thought as pleasure, the remembrance of an experience which has given great delight or sexual enjoyment? Is it the beauty of a sunset, or the delicate leaf that you touch or see, or the perfume of the flower that you smell? Is love pleasure, or desire? Or is it none of these? Is love to be divided as the sacred and the profane? Or is it something indivisible, whole, that cannot be broken up by thought? Does it exist without the object? Or does it come into being only because of the object? Is it because you see the face of a woman that love arises in you—love then being sensation, desire, pleasure, to which thought gives continuity? Or is love a state in you which responds to beauty as tenderness? Is love something cultivated by thought so that its object becomes important, or is it utterly unrelated to thought and, therefore, independent, free? Without understanding this word and the meaning behind it we shall be tortured, or become neurotic about sex, or be enslaved by it.

Love is not to be broken up into fragments by thought. When thought breaks it up into fragments, as impersonal, personal, sensuous, spiritual, my country and your country, my god and your god, then it is no longer love, then it is something entirely different—a product of memory, of propaganda, of convenience, of comfort and so on.

Is sex the product of thought? Is sex—the pleasure, the delight, the companionship, the tenderness involved in it—is this a remembrance strengthened by thought? In the sexual act there is self-forgetfulness, self-abandonment, a sense of the non-existence of fear, anxiety, the worries of life. Remembering this state of tenderness and self-forgetfulness, and demanding its repetition, you chew over it, as it were, until the next occasion. Is this tenderness, or is it merely a recollection of something that is over and which, through repetition, you hope to capture again? Is not the repetition of something, however pleasurable, a destructive process?

The young man suddenly found his tongue: "Sex is a biological urge, as you yourself have said, and if this is destructive then isn't eating equally destructive, because that also is a biological urge?"

If one eats when one is hungry—that is one thing. If one is hungry and thought says: "I must have the taste of this or that type of food"—then it is thought, and it is this which is the destructive repetition.

"In sex, how do you know what is the biological urge, like hunger, and what a psychological demand, like greed?" asked the young man.

Why do you divide the biological urge and the psychological demand? And there is yet another question, a different question altogether—why do you separate sex from seeing the beauty of a mountain or the loveliness of a flower? Why do you give such tremendous importance to the one and totally neglect the other?

"If sex is something quite different from love, as you seem to say, then is there any necessity at all to do anything about sex?" asked the young man.

We have never said that love and sex are two separate things. We have said that love is whole, not to be broken up, and thought, by its very nature, is fragmentary. When thought dominates, obviously there is no love. Man generally knows—perhaps only knows—the sex of thought, which is the chewing of the cud of pleasure and its repetition. Therefore we have to ask: Is there any other kind of sex which is not of thought or desire?

The sannyasi had listened to all this with quiet attention. Now he spoke: "I have resisted it, I have taken a vow against it, because by tradition, by reason, I have seen that one must have energy for the religious dedicated life. But I now see that this resistance has taken a great deal of energy. I have spent more time on resisting, and wasted more energy on it, than I have ever wasted on sex itself. So what you have said—that a conflict of any kind is a waste of energy— I now understand. Conflict and struggle are far more deadening than the seeing of a woman's face, or even perhaps than sex itself."

Is there love without desire, without pleasure? Is there sex, without desire, without pleasure? Is there love which is whole, without thought entering into it? Is sex something of the past, or is it something each time new? Thought is obviously old, so we are always contrasting the old and the new. We are asking questions from the old, and we want an answer in terms of the old. So when we ask: Is there sex without the whole mechanism of thought operating and working, doesn't it mean that we have not stepped out of the old? We are so conditioned by the old that we do not feel our way into the new. We said love is whole, and always new—new not as opposed to the old, for that again is the old. Any assertion that there is sex without desire is utterly valueless, but if you have followed the whole meaning of thought, then perhaps you will come upon the other. If, however, you demand that you must have your pleasure at any price, then love will not exist.

The young man said: "That biological urge you spoke about is precisely such a demand, for though it may be different from thought it engenders thought."

"Perhaps I can answer my young friend," said the

sannyasi, "for I have been through all this. I have trained myself for years not to look at a woman. I have ruthlessly controlled the biological demand. The biological urge does not engender thought; thought captures it, thought utilises it, thought makes images, pictures out of this urge—and then the urge is a slave to thought. It is thought which engenders the urge so much of the time. As I said, I am beginning to see the extraordinary nature of our own deception and dishonesty. There is a great deal of hypocrisy in us. We can never see things as they are but must create illusions about them. What you are telling us, sir, is to look at everything with clear eyes, without the memory of yesterday; you have repeated this so often in your talks. Then life does not become a problem. In my old age I am just beginning to realise this."

The young man looked not completely satisfied. He wanted life according to *his* terms, according to the formula which he had carefully built.

This is why it is very important to know oneself, not according to any formula or according to any guru. This constant choiceless awareness ends all illusions and all hypocrisy.

Now it was coming down in torrents, and the air was very still, and there was only the sound of the rain on the roof and on the leaves.

CALIFORNIA

MEDITATION IS NOT the mere experiencing of something beyond everyday thought and feeling nor is it the
pursuit of visions and delights. An immature and squalid
little mind can and does have visions of expanding consciousness, and experiences which it recognises according to its own
conditioning. This immaturity may be greatly capable of
making itself successful in this world and achieving fame
and notoriety. The gurus whom it follows are of the same
quality and state. Meditation does not belong to such as
these. It is not for the seeker, for the seeker finds what he
wants, and the comfort he derives from it is the morality of
his own fears.

Do what he will, the man of belief and dogma cannot
enter into the realm of meditation. To meditate, freedom is
necessary. It is not meditation first and freedom afterwards;
freedom—(the total denial of social morality) and values—is
the first movement of meditation. It is not a public affair
where many can join in and offer prayers. It stands alone,
and is always beyond the borders of social conduct. For
truth is not in the things of thought or in what thought has
put together and calls truth. The complete negation of this
whole structure of thought is the positive of meditation.

The sea was very calm that morning; it was very blue,
almost like a lake, and the sky was clear. Seagulls and pelicans were flying around the water's edge—the pelicans almost
touching the water, with their heavy wings and slow flight.
The sky was very blue and the hills beyond were sunburnt

except for a few bushes. A red eagle came out of those hills, flew over the gully and disappeared among the trees.

The light in that part of the world had a quality of penetration and brilliance, without blinding the eye. There was the smell of sumac, orange and eucalyptus. It hadn't rained for many months and the earth was parched, dry, cracked. You saw deer in the hills occasionally, and once, wandering up the hill there was a bear, dusty and ill-kempt. Along that path rattlers often went by and occasionally you saw a horned toad. On the trail you hardly passed anybody. It was a dusty, rocky and utterly silent trail.

Just in front of you was a quail with its chicks. There must have been more than a dozen of them, motionless, pretending they didn't exist. The higher you climbed the wilder it became for there was no habitation at all there, for there was no water. There were also no birds, and hardly any trees. The sun was very strong; it bit into you.

At that high altitude, suddenly, very close to you was a rattler, shrilly rattling his tail, giving a warning. You jumped. There it was, the rattler with its triangular head, all coiled up with its rattles in the centre and its head pointed towards you. You were a few feet away from it and it couldn't strike you from that distance. You stared at it, and it stared back with its unblinking eyes. You watched it for some time, its fat suppleness, its danger; and there was no fear. Then, as you watched, it uncoiled its head and tail towards you and moved backwards away from you. As you moved towards it, again it coiled, with its tail in the middle, ready to strike. You played this game for some time until the snake got tired and you left it and came down to the sea.

It was a nice house and the windows opened on to the lawn. The house was white inside and well-proportioned. On cold nights there was a fire. It is lovely to watch a fire with its thousand flames and many shadows. There was no noise, except the sound of the restless sea.

There was a small group of two or three in that room, talking about things in general—modern youth, the cinema, and so on. Then one of them said: "May we ask a question?" And it seemed a pity to disturb the blue sea and the hills. "We want to ask what time means to you. We know more or less what the scientists say about it, and the science-fiction writers. It seems to me that man has always been caught in this problem of time—the endless yesterdays and tomorrows. From the most remote periods to the present day, time has occupied man's mind. Philosophers have speculated about it, and religions have their own explanations. Can we talk about it?"

Shall we go into this matter rather deeply, or do you merely want to touch upon it superficially and let it go at that? If we want to talk about it seriously we must forget what religions, philosophers and others have said—for really you can't trust any of them. One doesn't distrust them just out of callous indifference or out of arrogance, but one sees that in order to find out, all authorities must be set aside. If one is prepared for that, then perhaps we could go into this matter very simply.

Is there—apart from the clock—time at all? We accept so many things; obedience has been so instilled into us that acceptance seems natural. But is there time at all, apart from the many yesterdays? Is time a continuity as yesterday, today and tomorrow, and is there time without yesterday? What gives to the thousand yesterdays a continuity?

A cause brings its effect, and the effect in turn becomes the cause; there is no division between them, it is one movement. This movement we call time, and with this movement, in our eyes and in our hearts, we see everything. We see with the eyes of time, and translate the present in terms of the past; and this translation meets the tomorrow. This is the chain of time.

Thought, caught in this process, asks the question: "What is time?" This very enquiry is of the machinery of time. So the enquiry has no meaning, for thought *is* time. The yesterday has produced thought and so thought divides space as yesterday, today and tomorrow. Or it says: "There is only the present", forgetting that the present itself is the outcome of yesterday.

Our consciousness is made up of this chain of time, and within its borders we are asking: "What is time? And, if there is no time, what happens to yesterday?" Such questions are within the field of time, and there is no answer to a question put by thought about time.

Or is there no tomorrow and no yesterday, but only the now? This question is not put by thought. It is put when the structure and nature of time is seen—but with the eyes of thought.

Is there actually tomorrow? Of course there is if I have to catch a train; but inwardly, is there the tomorrow of pain and pleasure, or of achievement? Or is there only the now, which is not related to yesterday? Time has a stop only when thought has a stop. It is at the moment of stopping that the now is. This now is not an idea, it is an actual fact, but only when the whole mechanism of thought has come to an end. The *feeling* of now is entirely different from the word, which is of time. So do not let us be caught in the words yesterday, today and tomorrow. The realisation of the now exists only in freedom, and freedom is not the cultivation of thought.

Then the question arises: "What is the action of the now?" We only know action which is of time and memory and the interval between yesterday and the present. In this interval or space all the confusion and the conflict begin.

What we are really asking is: If there is no interval at all, what is action? The conscious mind might say: "I did something spontaneously", but actually this is not so; there is no such thing as spontaneity because the mind is conditioned. The actual is the only fact; the actual is the now, and, unable to meet it, thought builds images about it. The interval between the image and what is, is the misery which thought has created.

To see what is without yesterday, is the now. The now is the silence of yesterday.

2

Meditation is a never-ending movement. You can never say that you are meditating or set aside a period for meditation. It isn't at your command. Its benediction doesn't come to you because you lead a systematised life or follow a particular routine or morality. It comes only when your heart is really open. Not opened by the key of thought, not made safe by the intellect, but when it is as open as the skies without a cloud; then it comes without your knowing, without your invitation. But you can never guard it, keep it, worship it. If you try, it will never come again: do what you will, it will avoid you. In meditation, you are not important, you have no place in it; the beauty of it is not you, but in itself. And to this you can add nothing. Don't look out of the window hoping to catch it unawares, or sit in a darkened room waiting for it; it comes only when you are not there at all, and its bliss has no continuity.

The mountains looked down on the endless blue sea, stretching out for miles. The hills were almost barren, sunburned, with small bushes, and in their folds there were trees, sunburned and fire-burned, but they were still there, flourishing and very quiet. There was one tree especially, an enormous old oak, that seemed to dominate all the hills around it. And on the top of another hill there was a dead tree, burnt by fire; there it stood naked, grey, without a single leaf. When you looked at those mountains, at their beauty and their lines against the blue sky, this tree alone was seen to hold the sky. It had many branches, all dead, and it would never feel the spring again. Yet it was intensely alive with grace and beauty; you felt you were part of it, alone with nothing to lean on, without time. It seemed it would be there for ever, like that big oak in the valley too. One was living and the other was dead, and both were the only things that mattered among these hills, sunburnt, scorched by the fire, waiting for the winter rains. You saw the whole of life, including your own life, in those two trees—one living, one dead. And love lay in between, sheltered, unseen, undemanding.

Under the house lived a mother with four of her young. The day we arrived they were there on the veranda, the mother racoon with her four babies. They were immediately friendly—with their sharp black eyes and soft paws— demanding to be fed and at the same time nervous. The mother was aloof. The next evening they were there again and they took their food from your hands and you felt their soft paws; they were ready to be tamed, to be petted. And you wondered at their beauty and their movement. In a few days they would be all over you, and you felt the immensity of life in them.

It was a lovely clear day and every little tree and bush stood out clearly against the bright sun. The man had come from the valley, up the hill to the house which overlooked a gully and, beyond it, a whole range of mountains. There were a few pines near the house and tall bamboos.

He was a young man full of hope, and the brutality of civilisation had not yet touched him. What he wanted was to sit quiet, to be silent, made silent not only by the hills but also by the quietness of his own urgency.

"What part do I play in this world? What is my relationship to the whole existing order? What is the meaning of this endless conflict? I have a love; we sleep together. And yet that is not the end. All this seems like a distant dream, fading and coming back, throbbing one moment, meaningless the next. I have seen some of my friends taking drugs. They have become stupid, dull-witted. Perhaps I too, even without drugs, will be made dull by the routine of life and the ache of my own loneliness. I don't count among these many millions of people. I shall go the way the others have gone, never coming upon a jewel that is incorruptible, that can never be stolen away, that can never tarnish. So I thought I'd come up here and talk to you, if you have the time. I'm not asking for any answers to my questions. I am perturbed: though I am very young I am already discouraged. I see the old, hopeless generation around me with their bitterness, cruelty, hypocrisy, compromise and prudence. They have nothing to give and, strangely enough, I don't want anything from them. I don't know what I want, but I do know that I must live a life that is very rich, that is full of meaning. I certainly don't want to enter some office and gradually become somebody in that shapeless, meaningless existence. I sometimes cry to myself at the loneliness and the beauty of the distant stars."

We sat quietly for some time, and the pine and the bamboo were caught in the breeze.

The lark and the eagle in their flight leave no mark; the scientist leaves a mark, as do all specialists. You can follow them step by step and add more steps to what they have found and accumulated; and you know, more or less, where their accumulation is leading. But truth is not like that; it is really a pathless land; it may be at the next curve of the road, or a thousand miles away. You have to keep going and then you will find it beside you. But if you stop and trace out a way for another to follow, or a design for your own way of life, it will never come near you.

"Is this poetic, or actual?"

What do you think? For us everything must be cut and dried so that we can do something practical with it, build something with it, worship it. You can bring a stick into the house, put it on a shelf, put a flower before it every day, and after some days the stick will have a great deal of meaning. The mind can give meaning to anything, but the meaning it gives is meaningless. When one asks what is the purpose of life, it's like worshipping that stick. The terrible thing is that the mind is always inventing new purposes, new meanings, new delights, and always destroying them. It is never quiet. A mind that is rich in its quietness never looks beyond what is. One must be both the eagle and the scientist, knowing well that the two can never meet. This doesn't mean that they are two separate things. Both are necessary. But when the scientist wants to become the eagle, and when the eagle leaves its footprints, there is misery in the world.

You are quite young. Don't ever lose your innocency and the vulnerability that it brings. That is the only treasure that man can have, and must have.

"Is this vulnerability the be-all and end-all of existence? Is it the only priceless jewel that can be discovered?"

You can't be vulnerable without innocency, and though you have a thousand experiences, a thousand smiles and tears, if you don't die to them, how can the mind be innocent? It is only the innocent mind—in spite of its thousand experiences—that can see what truth is. And it is only truth that makes the mind vulnerable—that is, free.

"You say you can't see truth without being innocent, and you can't be innocent without seeing truth. This is a vicious circle, isn't it?"

Innocency can be only with the death of yesterday. But we never die to yesterday. We always have a remnant, a tattered part of yesterday remaining, and it is this that keeps the mind anchored, held by time. So time is the enemy of innocency. One must die every day to everything that the mind has captured and holds on to. Otherwise there is no freedom. In freedom there is vulnerability. It is not the one thing after the other—it is all one movement, both the coming and the going. It is really the fullness of heart that is innocent.

3

Meditation is emptying the mind of the known. The known is the past. The emptying is not at the end of accumulation but rather it means not to accumulate at all. What has been is emptied only in the present, not by thought but by action, by the doing of what is. The past is the movement of conclusion to conclusion, and the judgment of what is by the conclusion. All judgment is conclusion, whether it be of the past or of the present, and it is this conclusion that prevents the constant emptying of the mind of the known; for the known is always conclusion, determination.

The known is the action of will, and the will in operation is the continuation of the known, so the action of will cannot possibly empty the mind. The empty mind cannot be purchased at the altar of demand; it comes into being when thought is aware of its own activities—not the thinker being aware of his thought.

Meditation is the innocency of the present, and therefore it is always alone. The mind that is completely alone,

untouched by thought, ceases to accumulate. So the emptying of the mind is always in the present. For the mind that is
alone, the future—which is of the past—ceases. Meditation
is a movement, not a conclusion, not an end to be achieved.

The forest was very large, with pine trees, oaks, shrubs
and redwood. There was a little stream that went by down
the slope, making a constant murmuring. There were butter-
flies, small ones, blue and yellow, which seemed to find no
flowers to rest on, and they drifted down towards the valley.
This forest was very old, and the redwoods were older still.
They were enormous trees of great height, and there was
that peculiar atmosphere which comes when man is absent—
with his guns, his chattering and the display of his knowledge. There was no road through the forest. You had to
leave the car at some distance and walk along a track covered
with pine needles.
There was a jay, warning everybody of human approach.
The warning had effect, for all animal movement seemed to
stop, and there was that feeling of the intensity of watching.
It was difficult for the sun to penetrate here, and there was a
stillness which you could almost touch.
Two red squirrels, with long bushy tails, came down the
pine tree, chattering, their claws making a scratching sound.
They chased each other round and round the trunk, up and
down, with a fury of pleasure and delight. There was a tension between them—the chord of play, of sex, and fun. They
were really enjoying themselves. The top one would suddenly stop and watch the lower one who was still in movement, then the lower one too would stop, and they would
look at each other, with their tails up and their noses twitch-
ing, pointed towards each other. Their sharp eyes were taking each other in, and also the movement around them. They
had scolded the watcher, sitting under the tree, and now they

had forgotten him; but they were aware of each other, and you could almost feel their utter delight in each other's company. Their nest must have been high up, and presently they got tired; one ran up the tree and the other along the ground, disappearing behind another tree.

The jay, blue, sharp and curious, had been watching them and the man sitting under the tree, and he too flew off, loudly calling.

There were clouds coming up and probably in an hour or two there would be a thunderstorm.

She was an analyst with a degree, and was working in a large clinic. She was quite young, in modern dress, the skirt right above the knee; she seemed very intense, and you could see that she was very disturbed. At the table she was unnecessarily talkative, expressing strongly what she thought about things, and it seemed that she never looked out of the big window at the flowers, the breeze among the leaves, and the tall, heavy eucalyptus, gently swaying in the wind. She ate haphazardly, not particularly interested in what she was eating.

In the adjoining small room, she said : "We analysts help sick people to fit into a sicker society and we sometimes, perhaps very rarely, succeed. But actually any success is nature's own accomplishment. I have analysed many people. I don't like what I am doing, but I have to earn a living, and there are so many sick people. I don't believe one can help them very much, though of course we are always trying new drugs, chemicals and theories. But apart from the sick, I am myself struggling to be different—different from the ordinary average person."

Aren't you, in your very struggle to be different, the same as the others? And why all this struggle?

"But if I don't struggle, fight, I'll be just like the ordinary bourgeois housewife. I want to be different, and that's why I don't want to marry. But I am really very lonely, and my loneliness has pushed me into this work."

So this loneliness is gradually leading you to suicide, isn't it?

She nodded; she was almost in tears.

Isn't the whole movement of consciousness leading to isolation, to fear, and to this incessant struggle to be different? It is all part of this urge to fulfil, to identify oneself with something, or to identify oneself with what one is. Most of the analysts have their teachers according to whose theories and established schools they operate, merely modifying them and adding a new twist to them.

"I belong to the new school; we approach without the symbol and face reality actually. We have discarded the former masters with their symbols and we see the human being as he is. But all this is something that is also becoming another school, and I am not here to discuss various types of schools, theories and masters, but rather to talk about myself. I don't know what to do."

Are you not just as sick as the patients whom you are trying to cure? Aren't you part of society—which is perhaps more confused and more sick than yourself? So the issue is more fundamental, isn't it?

You are the result of this enormous weight of society, with its culture and its religions, and it is driving you, both economically and inwardly. Either you have to make your peace with society, which is to accept its maladies and live with them, or totally refute it, and find a new way of living. But you can't find the new way without letting go of the old.

What you really want is security, isn't it? That's the whole search of thought—to be different, to be more clever, more sharp, more ingenious. In this process you are trying to find a deep security, aren't you? But is there such a thing at all? Security denies order. There is no security in relationship, in belief, in action, and because one is seeking it one creates disorder. Security breeds disorder, and when you face the ever-mounting disorder in yourself, you want to end it all.

Within the area of consciousness with its wide and narrow frontiers, thought is ever trying to find a secure spot. So thought is creating disorder; order is not the outcome of thought. When disorder ends there is order. Love is not within the regions of thought. Like beauty, it cannot be touched by the paintbrush. One has to abandon the total disorder of oneself.

She became very silent, withdrawn into herself. It was difficult for her to control the tears that were coming down her cheeks.

4

Sleep is as important as keeping awake, perhaps more so. If during the day time the mind is watchful, self-recollected, observing the inward and outward movement of life, then at night meditation comes as a benediction. The mind wakes up, and out of the depth of silence there is the enchantment of meditation, which no imagination or flight of fancy can ever bring about. It happens without the mind ever inviting it : it comes into being out of the tranquillity of consciousness —not within it but outside of it, not in the periphery of thought but beyond the reaches of thought. So there is no memory of it, for remembrance is always of the past, and meditation is not the resurrection of the past. It happens out of the fullness of the heart and not out of intellectual brightness and capacity. It may happen night after night, but each time, if you are so blessed, it is new—not new in being different from old, but new without the background of the old, new in its diversity and changeless change. So sleep becomes a thing of extraordinary importance, not the sleep of exhaustion, not the sleep brought about through drugs and physical satisfaction, but a sleep that is as light and quick as the body is sensitive. And the body is made sensitive through alertness. Sometimes meditation is as light as a breeze that passes by; at other times its depth is beyond all measure. But if the mind holds one or the other as a remembrance to be indulged in, then the ecstasy of meditation comes to an end. It is important never to possess or desire possession of it. The quality of possessiveness must never enter into meditation, for meditation has no root, nor any substance which the mind can hold.

The other day as we went up the deep canyon which lay in shadow with the arid mountains on both sides, it was full of birds, insects, and the quiet activity of small animals. You walked up and up the gentle slope to a great height, and from there you watched all the surrounding hills and mountains with the light of the setting sun upon them. It looked as though they were lit from within, never to be put out. But as you watched, the light faded, and in the west the evening star became brighter and brighter. It was a lovely evening, and somehow you felt that the whole universe was there beside you, and a strange quietness surrounded you.

We have no light within ourselves: we have the artificial light of others; the light of knowledge, the light that talent and capacity give. All this kind of light fades and becomes a pain. The light of thought becomes its own shadow. But the light that never fades, the deep, inward brilliance which is not a thing of the market place, cannot be shown to another. You can't seek it, you can't cultivate it, you can't possibly imagine it or speculate upon it, for it is not within the reach of the mind.

He was a monk of some repute, having lived both in a

monastery and alone outside it, seeking, and deeply earnest.

"The things you say about meditation seem true; it is out of reach. This means, doesn't it, that there must be no seeking, no wishing, no gesture of any kind towards it, whether the deliberate gesture of sitting in a special posture, or the gesture of an attitude towards life or towards oneself? So what is one to do? What is the point of any words at all?"

You seek out of emptiness, reach out either to fill that emptiness or to escape from it. This outward movement from inward poverty is conceptual, speculative, dualistic. This is conflict, and it is endless. So don't reach out! But the energy which was reaching out turns from reaching out to reaching inwards, seeking and searching, asking something which it now calls "within". The two movements are essentially the same. They must both come to an end.

"Are you asking us simply to be content with this emptiness?"

Certainly not.

"So the emptiness remains, and a settled kind of despair. The despair is even greater if one may not even seek!"

Is it despair if you see the truth that the inward and outward movement have no meaning? Is it contentment with what is? Is it the acceptance of this emptiness? It is none of these. So: you have dispelled the going out, the coming in, the accepting. You have denied all movement of the mind that is faced with this emptiness. Then the mind itself is empty, for the movement is the mind itself. The mind is empty of all movement, therefore there is no entity to initiate any movement. Let it remain empty. Let it *be* empty. The mind has purged itself of the past, the future and the present; it has purged itself of becoming, and becoming is time. So there is no time; there is no measurement. *Then* is it emptiness?

"This state comes and goes often. Even if it is not empti-ness, it is certainly not the ecstasy of which you speak."

Forget what has been said. Forget also that it comes and goes. When it comes and goes it is of time; then there is the observer who says, "It is here, it has gone". This observer is the one who measures, compares, evaluates, so it is not the emptiness of which we are talking.

"Are you anaesthetising me?" And he laughed.

When there is no measurement and no time, is there a frontier or an outline to emptiness? Then can you ever call it emptiness or nothingness? Then everything is in it, and nothing is in it.

5

It had been raining quite a bit during the night, and now, early in the morning as you were getting up, there was the strong smell of sumac, sage, and damp earth. It was red earth, and red earth seems to give a stronger smell than brown earth. Now the sun was on the hills with that extraordinary colour of burnt-sienna, and every tree and every bush was sparkling, washed clean by last night's rain, and everything was burst-ing with joy. It hadn't rained for six or eight months, and you can imagine how the earth was rejoicing, and not only the earth but everything on it—the huge trees, the tall eucalyptus, the pepper trees and the live-oaks. The birds seemed to have a different song that morning, and as you watched the hills and the distant blue mountains, you were somehow lost in them. You didn't exist, neither did those around you. There was only this beauty, this immensity, only the spreading, widening earth. That morning, out of those hills that went on for miles and miles, came a tranquillity which met your own quietness. It was like the earth and the heavens meeting, and the ecstasy was a benediction.

The same evening, as you walked up the canyon into the hills, the red earth was damp under your feet, soft, yielding, and full of promise. You went up the steep incline for many miles, and then came down suddenly. As you turned the corner you came upon that complete silence which was already descending on you, and as you entered the deep valley it became more penetrating, more urgent, more insistent. There was no thought, only that silence. As you walked down, it seemed to cover the whole earth, and it was astonishing how every bird and tree became still. There was no breeze among the trees and with the darkness they were withdrawing into their solitude. It is strange how during the day they would welcome you, and now, with their fantastic shapes, they were distant, aloof and withdrawn. Three hunters went by with their powerful bows and arrows, electric torches strapped to their foreheads. They were out to kill the night birds and seemed to be utterly impervious to the beauty and the silence about them. They were intent only on the kill, and it seemed as though everything was watching them, horrified, and full of pity.

That morning a group of young people had come to the house. There were about thirty of them, students from various universities. They had grown up in this climate, and were strong, well fed, tall, and enthusiastic. Only one or two of them sat on chairs, most of us were on the floor, and the girls in their mini-skirts sat uncomfortably. One of the boys spoke, with quivering lips, and with his head down.

"I want to live a different kind of life. I don't want to be caught in sex and drugs and the rat race. I want to live out of this world, and yet I am caught in it. I have sex, and the next day I am utterly depressed. I know I want to live peacefully, with love in my heart, but I am torn by my urges, by the pull of the society in which I live. I want to obey these urges, yet I rebel against them. I want to live at the mountain top yet I am always descending into the valley, for my life is there. I don't know what to do. I'm getting bored with everything. My parents can't help me, nor can the professors with whom I sometimes try to discuss these matters. They are as confused and miserable as I am, more so in fact, because they are much older."

What is important is not to come to any conclusion, or any decision for or against sex, not to get caught in conceptual ideologies. Let us look at the whole picture of our existence. The monk has taken a vow of celibacy because he thinks that to gain his heaven he has to shun contact with a woman; but for the rest of his life he is struggling against his own physical demands: he is in conflict with heaven and with earth, and spends the rest of his days in darkness, seeking light. Each one of us is caught in this ideological battle, just like the monk, burning with desire and trying to suppress it for the promise of heaven. We have a physical body and it has its demands. They are encouraged and influenced by the society in which we live, by the advertisements, by the half-naked girls, by the insistence on fun, amusement, entertainment, and by the morality of society, the morality of the social order, which is disorder and immorality. We are physically stimulated—more and tastier food, drink, television. The whole of modern existence focuses your attention on sex. You are stimulated in every way—by books, by talk, and by an utterly permissive society. All this surrounds you; it's no good merely shutting your eyes to it. You have to see this whole way of life with its absurd beliefs and divisions, and the utter meaninglessness of a life spent in an office or a factory. And at the end of it all there is death. You have to see all this confusion very clearly.

Now look out of that window and see those marvellous mountains, freshly washed by last night's rain, and that extraordinary light of California which exists nowhere else. See the beauty of the light on those hills. You can smell the clean air and the newness of the earth. The more alive you are to it, the more sensitive you are to all this immense, incredible light and beauty, the more you are with it—the more your perception is heightened. That is also sensuous, just like seeing a girl. You can't respond with your senses to this mountain and then cut them off when you see the girl; in this way you divide life, and in this division there is sorrow and conflict. When you divide the mountain-top from the valley, you are in conflict. This doesn't mean that you avoid conflict or escape from it, or get so lost in sex or some other appetite that you cut yourself off from conflict. The understanding of conflict doesn't mean that you vegetate or become like a cow.

To understand all this is not to be caught in it, not to depend on it. It means never to deny anything, never to come to any conclusion or to reach any ideological, verbal state, or principle, according to which you try to live. The very perception of this whole map which is being unfolded is already intelligence. It is this intelligence that will act and not a conclusion, a decision or an ideological principle.

Our bodies have been made dull, just as our minds and hearts have been dulled, by our education, by our conformity to the pattern which society has set and which denies the sensitivity of the heart. It sends us to war, destroying all our beauty, tenderness and joy. The observation of all this, not verbally or intellectually but actually, makes our body and mind highly sensitive. The body will then demand the right kind of food; then the mind will not be caught in words, in symbols, in platitudes of thought. Then we shall know how to live both in the valley and on the mountain-top; then there will be no division or contradiction between the two.

EUROPE

I

MEDITATION IS A movement in attention. Attention is not an achievement, for it is not personal. The personal element comes in only when there is the observer as the centre, from which he concentrates or dominates; thus all achievement is fragmentary and limited. Attention has no border, no frontier to cross; attention is clarity, clear of all thought. Thought can never make for clarity for thought has its roots in the dead past; so thinking is an action in the dark. Awareness of this is to be attentive. Awareness is not a method that leads to attention; such attention is within the field of thought and so can be controlled or modified; being aware of this inattention is attention. Meditation is not an intellectual process—which is still within the area of thought. Meditation is the freedom from thought, and a movement in the ecstasy of truth.

It was snowing that morning. A bitter wind was blowing; and the movement upon the trees was a cry for spring. In that light, the trunks of the large beech and the elm had that peculiar quality of grey-green that one finds in old woods where the earth is soft and covered with autumn leaves. Walking among them you had the feeling of the wood —not of the separate individual trees with their particular shapes and forms—but rather of the entire quality of all the trees.

Suddenly the sun came out, and there was a vast blue sky towards the east, and a dark, heavily-laden sky against the west. In that moment of bright sunlight, spring began. In the quiet stillness of the spring day you felt the beauty of the earth and the sense of unity of the earth and all things upon it. There was no separation between you and the tree and the varying, astonishing colours of the sparkling light on the holly. You, the observer, had ceased, and so the division, as space and time, had come to an end.

He said he was a religious man—not belonging to any particular organisation or belief—but he felt religious. Of course he had been through the drill of talking with all the religious leaders, and had come away from them all rather despairingly, but without becoming a cynic. Yet he had not found the bliss he sought. He had been a professor at a university, and had given it up to lead a life of meditation and enquiry.

"You know," he said, "I am always aware of the fragmentation of life. I, myself, am a fragment of that life—broken, different, endlessly struggling to become the whole, an integral part of this universe. I have tried to find my own identity, for modern society is destroying all identity. I wonder if there is a way out of all this division into something that cannot be divided, separated?"

We have divided life as the family and the community, the family and the nation, the family and the office, politics and the religious life, peace and war, order and disorder—an endless division of the opposites. Along this corridor we walk, trying to bring about a harmony between mind and heart, trying to keep a balance between love and envy. We know all this too well, and we try to make out of it some kind of harmony.

What makes this division? Obviously there *is* division, contrast—black and white, man and woman, and so on—but what is the source, the essence, of this fragmentation? Unless we find it, fragmentation is inevitable. What do you think is the root cause of this duality?

"I can give many causes for this seemingly endless division, and many ways in which one has tried to build a bridge between opposites. Intellectually I can expose the reasons for this division, but it leads nowhere. I have played this game often, with myself and with others. I have tried, through meditation, through the exercise of will, to feel the unity of things, to be one with everything—but it is a barren attempt."

Of course the mere discovery of the cause of the separation does not necessarily dissolve it. One knows the cause of fear, but one is still afraid. The intellectual exploration loses its immediacy of action when the sharpness of thought is all that matters. The fragmentation of the I and the not-I is surely the basic cause of this division, though the I tries to identify itself with the not-I, which may be the wife, the family, the community, or the formula of God which thought has made. The I is ever striving to find an identity, but what it identifies itself with is still a concept, a memory, a structure of thought.

Is there a duality at all? Objectively there is, such as light and shade, but psychologically is there? We accept the psychological duality as we accept the objective duality; it is part of our conditioning. We never question this conditioning. But is there, psychologically, a division? There is only what is, not what should be. The what should be is a division which thought has put together in the avoiding or the overcoming of the reality of what is. Hence the struggle between the actual and the abstraction. The abstraction is the fanciful, the romantic, the ideal. What is actual is what is, and everything else is non-real. It is the non-real that brings about the fragmentation, not the actual. Pain is actual; non-pain is the pleasure of thought which brings about the division between the pain and the state of non-pain. Thought is always separative; it is the division of time, the space between the observer and the thing observed. There is only what is, and to see what is, without thought as the observer, is the ending of fragmentation.

Thought is not love; but thought, as pleasure, encloses love and brings pain within that enclosure. In the negation of what is not, what is remains. In the negation of what is not love, love emerges in which the I and the non-I cease.

2

Innocency and spaciousness are the flowering of meditation. There is no innocency without space. Innocency is not immaturity. You may be mature physically, but the vast space that comes with love is not possible if the mind is not free from the many marks of experience. It is these scars of experience that prevent innocency. Freeing the mind from the constant pressure of experience is meditation.

Just as the sun is setting there comes a strange quietness and a feeling that everything about you has come to an end, though the bus, the taxi and the noise go on. This sense of aloofness seems to penetrate the whole universe. You must have felt this too. Often it comes most unexpectedly; strange stillness and peace seem to pour down from the heavens and cover the earth. It is a benediction, and the beauty of the evening is made boundless by it. The shiny road after the rain, the waiting cars, the empty park, seem to be part of it; and the laughter of the couple who pass by does not in any way disturb the peace of the evening.

The naked trees, black against the sky, with their delicate branches, were waiting for the spring, and it was just round the corner, hastening to meet them. There was already new grass, and the fruit trees were in bloom. The country was slowly becoming alive again, and from this hill-top you could see the city with many, many domes, and one more haughty and higher than the others. You could see the flat tops of the pine trees, and the evening light was upon the clouds. The whole horizon seemed to be filled with these clouds, range after range, piling up against the hills in the most fantastic shapes, castles such as man had never built. There were deep chasms and towering peaks. All these clouds were alight with a dark red glow and a few of them seemed to be afire, not by the sun, but within themselves.

These clouds didn't make the space; they were in the space, which seemed to stretch infinitely, from eternity to eternity.

A blackbird was singing in a bush close by, and that was the everlasting blessing.

There were three or four who had brought their wives and we all sat on the floor. From this position the windows were too high for one to see the garden or the wall opposite. They were all professionals. One said he was a scientist, another a mathematician, another, an engineer; they were specialists, not overflowing beyond their boundaries—as the river does after heavy rain. It is the overflowing that enriches the soil.

The engineer asked: "You have often talked about space and we are all interested to know what you mean by it. The bridge covers the space between two banks or between two hills. Space is made by a dam which is filled by water. There is space between us and the expanding universe. There is space between you and me. Is this what you mean?"

The others seconded the question; they must have talked it over before they came. One said: "I could put it differently, in more scientific terms, but it comes to more or less the same thing."

There is space that divides and encloses, and space that is unlimited. The space between man and man, in which grows mischief is the limited space of division; there is division between you as you are and the image you have about yourself; there is division between you and your wife; there is division between what you are and the ideal of what you should be; there is division between hill and hill. And there is the beauty of space that is without the boundary of time and line.

Is there space between thought and thought? Between remembrances? Between actions? Or is there no space at all between thought and thought? Between reason and reason? Between health and ill-health—cause becoming the effect, and the effect becoming the cause?

If there were a break between thought and thought, then thought would be always new, but because there is no break, no space, all thought is old. You may not be conscious of the continuity of a thought; you may pick it up a week later after dropping it, but it has been working within the old boundaries.

So the whole of consciousness, both the conscious and the unconscious—which is an unfortunate word to have to use— is within the limited, narrow space of tradition, culture, custom and remembrance. Technology may take you to the moon, you may build a curving bridge over a chasm or bring some order within the limited space of society, but this again will breed disorder.

Space exists not only beyond the four walls of this room; there is also the space which the room makes. There is the enclosing space, the sphere, which the observer creates around himself through which he sees the observed—which also creates a sphere around itself.

When the observer looks at the stars of an evening, his space is limited. He may be able, through a telescope, to see many thousands of light years away, but he is the maker of space and therefore it is finite. The measurement between the observer and the observed is space, and time to cover that space.

There is not only physical space but the psychological dimension in which thought covers itself—as yesterday, today and tomorrow. So long as there is an observer, space is the narrow yard of the prison in which there is no freedom at all.

"But we'd like to ask if you are trying to convey space without the observer? That seems to be utterly impossible, or it might be a fancy of your own."

Freedom, sir, is not within the prison, however comfortable and decorated it may be. If one has a dialogue with freedom it cannot possibly exist within the boundaries of memory, knowledge and experience. Freedom demands that you break the prison walls, though you may enjoy the limited disorder, the limited slavery, the toil within this boundary.

Freedom is not relative; either there is freedom or there is not. If there is not, then one must accept the narrow, limited life with its conflicts, sorrows and aches—merely bringing about a little change here and there.

Freedom is infinite space. When there is a lack of space there is violence—as with the predator, and the bird who claims his space, his territory, for which he will fight. This violence may be relative under the law and the policeman just as the limited space the predators and the birds demand, for which they will fight, is limited violence. Because of the limited space between man and man aggression must exist.

"Are you trying to tell us, sir, that man will always be in conflict within himself and with the world so long as he lives within the sphere of his own making?"

Yes, sir. So we come to the central issue of freedom. Within the narrow culture of society there is no freedom, and because there is no freedom there is disorder. Living within this disorder man seeks freedom in ideologies, in theories, in what he calls God. This escape is not freedom. It is the yard of the prison again which separates man from man. Can thought, which has brought this conditioning upon itself, come to an end, break down this structure, and go beyond and above it? Obviously it cannot, and that is the first factor to see. The intellect cannot possibly build a bridge between itself and freedom. Thought, which is the response of memory, experience and knowledge, is always old, as is the intellect, and the old cannot build a bridge to the new. Thought is essentially the observer with his prejudices, fears and anxieties, and this thinking-image—because of his isolation—obviously makes a sphere around himself. Thus there is a distance between the observer and the observed. The observer tries to establish a relationship preserving this distance—and so there is conflict and violence.

In all this there is no fancy. Imagination in any form destroys truth. Freedom is beyond thought; freedom means infinite space not created by the observer. Coming upon this freedom is meditation.

There is no space without silence, and silence is not put together by time as thought. Time will never give freedom; order is possible only when the heart is not covered over with words.

3

A meditative mind is silent. It is not the silence which thought can conceive of; it is not the silence of a still evening; it is the silence when thought—with all its images, its words and perceptions—has entirely ceased. This meditative mind is the religious mind—the religion that is not touched by the church, the temples or by chants.

The religious mind is the explosion of love. It is this love that knows no separation. To it, far is near. It is not the one or the many, but rather that state of love in which all division ceases. Like beauty, it is not of the measure of words. From this silence alone the meditative mind acts.

It had rained the day before and in the evening the sky had been full of clouds. In the distance the hills were covered with clouds of delight, full of light, and as you watched them they were taking different shapes.

The setting sun, with its golden light, was touching only one or two mountains of cloud, but those clouds seemed as solid as the dark cypress. As you looked at them you naturally became silent. The vast space and the solitary tree on the hill, the distant dome, and the talking going on around one —were all part of this silence. You knew that the next morning it would be lovely, for the sunset was red. And it was lovely; there wasn't a cloud in the sky and it was very blue. The yellow flowers and the white flowering tree against the dark hedge of cypress, and the smell of spring, filled the land. The dew was on the grass, and slowly spring was coming out of darkness.

He said he had just lost his son who had had a very good job and who would soon have become one of the directors of a large company. He was still under the shock of it, but he had great control over himself. He wasn't the type that cried —tears would not come to him easily. He had been schooled all his life by hard work in a matter-of-fact technology. He was not an imaginative man, and the complex, subtle, psychological problems of life had hardly touched him.

The recent death of his son was an unacknowledged blow. He said: "It is a sad event."

This sadness was a terrible thing for his wife and children. "How can I explain to them the ending of sorrow, of which you have talked? I myself have studied and perhaps can understand it, but what of the others who are involved in it?"

Sorrow is in every house, round every corner. Every human being has this engulfing grief, caused by so many incidents and accidents. Sorrow seems like an endless wave that comes upon man, almost drowning him; and the pity of sorrow breeds bitterness and cynicism.

Is the sorrow for your son, or for yourself, or for the break in the continuity of yourself through your son? Is there the sorrow of self-pity? Or is there sorrow because he was so promising in the worldly sense?

If it is self-pity, then this self-concern, this isolating factor in life—though there is the outward semblance of relationship—must inevitably cause misery. This isolating process, this activity of self-concern in everyday life, this ambition, this pursuit of one's own self-importance, this separative way of living, whether one is aware of it or not, must bring about the loneliness from which we try to escape in so many different ways. Self-pity is the ache of loneliness, and this pain is called sorrow.

Then there is also the sorrow of ignorance—not the ignorance of the lack of books or of technical knowledge or the lack of experience, but the ignorance we have accepted as time, as evolution, the evolution from what is to what should be—the ignorance which makes us accept authority with all its violence, the ignorance of conformity with its dangers and pains, the ignorance of not knowing the whole structure of oneself. This is the sorrow that man has spread wherever he has been.

So we must be clear about what it is that we call sorrow—

sorrow being grief, the loss of what was the supposed good, the sorrow of insecurity and the constant demand for security. Which is it that you are caught in? Unless this is clear there is no ending to sorrow.

This clarity is not a verbal explanation nor is it the result of a clever intellectual analysis. You must be aware, of what your sorrow is as clearly as you become aware, sensually, when you touch that flower.

Without understanding this whole way of sorrow, how can you end it? You can escape from it by going to the temple or the church or taking to drink—but all escapes, whether to God or to sex, are the same, for they do not solve sorrow.

So you have to lay down the map of sorrow and trace every path and road. If you allow time to cover this map, then time will strengthen the brutality of sorrow. You have to see this whole map at a glance—seeing the whole and then the detail, not the detail first and then the whole. In ending sorrow, time must come to an end.

Sorrow cannot end by thought. When time stops, thought as the way of sorrow, ceases. It is thought and time that divide and separate, and love is not thought or time.

See the map of sorrow not with the eyes of memory. Listen to the whole murmur of it; be of it, for you are both the observer and the observed. Then only can sorrow end. There is no other way.

4

Meditation is never prayer. Prayer, supplication, is born of self-pity. You pray when you are in difficulty, when there is sorrow; but when there is happiness, joy, there is no supplication. This self-pity, so deeply embedded in man, is the root of separation. That which is separate, or thinks itself separate, ever seeking identification with something which is not separate, brings only more division and pain. Out of this confusion one cries to heaven, or to one's husband, or to some deity of the mind. This cry may find an answer, but the answer is the echo of self-pity, in its separation.

The repetition of words, of prayers, is self-hypnotic, self-enclosing and destructive. The isolation of thought is always within the field of the known, and the answer to prayer is the response of the known.

Meditation is far from this. In that field, thought cannot enter; there is no separation, and so no identity. Meditation is in the open; secrecy has no place in it. Everything is exposed, clear; then the beauty of love is.

It was an early spring morning with a few flakey clouds moving gently across the blue sky from the west. A cock began to crow, and it was strange to hear it in a crowded town. It began early, and for nearly two hours it kept announcing the arrival of the day. The trees were still empty, but there were thin, delicate leaves against the clear morning sky.

If you were very quiet, without any thought flashing across the mind, you could just hear the deep bell of some cathedral. It must have been far away, and in the short silences between the cock's crowing you could hear the waves of this sound coming towards you and going beyond you—you almost rode on them, going far away, disappearing into the immensities. The crowing of the cock and the deep sound of the distant bell had a strange effect. The noises of the town had not yet begun. There was nothing to interrupt the clear sound. You didn't hear it with your ears, you heard it with your heart, not with thought that knows "the bell" and "the cock", and it was pure sound. It came out of silence and your heart picked it up and went with it from everlasting to everlasting. It was not an organised sound, like music; it was not the sound of silence between two notes; it was not the sound you hear when you have stopped talking. All such sounds are heard by the mind or by the ear. When you hear with your heart, the world is filled with it and your eyes see clearly.

She was quite a young lady, well turned out, her hair cut short, highly efficient and capable. From what she said she had no illusions about herself. She had children and a certain quality of seriousness. Perhaps she was somewhat romantic and very young, but for her the Orient had lost its aura of mysticism—which was just as well. She talked simply, without any hesitation.

"I think I committed suicide a long time ago, when a certain event took place in my life; with that event my life ended. Of course I have carried on outwardly, with the children and all the rest of it, but I have stopped living."

Don't you think that most people, knowingly or unknowingly, are always committing suicide? The extreme form of it is jumping out of the window. But it begins, probably, when there is the first resistance and frustration. We build a wall around ourselves behind which we lead our own separate lives—though we may have husbands, wives and children. This separative life is the life of suicide, and that is the accepted morality of religion and society. The acts of separation are of a continuous chain and lead to war and to self-destruction. Separation is suicide, whether of the individual or of the community or of the nation. Each one wants to live a life of self-identity, of self-centred activity, of the self-enclosing sorrow of conformity. It is suicide when belief and dogma hold you by the hand. Before the event, you invested your life and the whole movement of it in the one against the many, and when the one dies, or the god is destroyed, your life goes with it and you have nothing to live for. If you are terribly clever you invent a meaning to life—which the experts have always done—but having committed yourself to that meaning you are already committing suicide. All commitment is self-destruction, whether it be in the name of God or in the name of Socialism, or anything else.

You, madam—and this is not said in cruelty—ceased to exist because you could not get what you wanted; or it was taken away from you; or you wanted to go through a particular, special door which was tightly shut. As sorrow and pleasure are self-enclosing, so acceptance and insistence bring their own darkness of separation. We do not live, we are always committing suicide. Living begins when the act of suicide ends.

"I understand what you mean. I see what I have done. But now what am I to do? How am I to come back from the long years of death?"

You can't come back; if you came back you would follow the old pattern, and sorrow would pursue you as a cloud is driven by the wind. The only thing you can do is to see that to lead one's own life, separately, in secret, demanding the continuity of pleasure—is to invite the separation of death. In separation there is no love. Love has no identity. Pleasure, and the seeking of it, build the enclosing wall of separation. There is no death when all commitment ceases. Self-knowledge is the open door.

5

Meditation is the ending of the word. Silence is not induced by a word, the word being thought. The action out of silence is entirely different from the action born of the word; meditation is the freeing of the mind from all symbols, images and remembrances.

That morning the tall poplars with their fresh, new leaves were playing in the breeze. It was a spring morning and the hills were covered with flowering almonds, cherries and apples. The whole earth was tremendously alive. The cypresses were stately and aloof, but the flowering trees were touching, branch to branch, and rows of poplars were casting swaying shadows. Beside the road there was running water which would eventually become the old river.

There was scent in the air, and every hill was different from the others. On some of them stood houses surrounded by olives and rows of cypresses leading to the house. The road wound through all these soft hills.

It was a sparkling morning, full of intense beauty, and the powerful car was somehow not out of place. There seemed to be extraordinary order, but, of course, inside each house there was disorder—man plotting against man, children crying or laughing; the whole chain of misery was stretching unseen from house to house. Spring, autumn and winter never broke this chain.

But that morning there was a rebirth. Those tender leaves never knew the winter nor the coming autumn; they were vulnerable and therefore innocent.

From the window one could see the old dome of the striped marble cathedral and the many-coloured campanile; and within were the dark symbols of sorrow and hope. It was really a lovely morning, but strangely there were few birds, for here people kill them for sport, and their song was very still.

He was an artist, a painter. He said he had a talent for it as another might have a talent for the building of bridges.

He had long hair, delicate hands and was enclosed within the dream of his own gifts. He would come out of it—talk, explain—and then go back into his own den. He said his pictures were selling and he had had several one-man exhibitions. He was rather proud of this, and his voice told of it.

There is the army, within its own walls of self-interest; and the business-man enclosed within steel and glass; and the housewife pottering about the house waiting for her husband and her children. There is the museum-keeper, and the orchestra conductor, each living within a fragment of life, each fragment becoming extraordinarily important, unrelated, in contradiction to other fragments, having its own honours, its own social dignity, its own prophets. The religious fragment is unrelated to the factory, and the factory to the artist; the general is unrelated to the soldiers, as the priest is to the layman. Society is made up of these fragments, and the do-gooder and the reformer are trying to patch up the broken pieces. But through these separative, broken, specialised parts, the human being carries on with his anxieties, guilt and apprehensions. In that we are all related, not in our specialised fields.

In the common greed, hate and aggression, human beings are related and this violence builds the culture, the society, in which we live. It is the mind and the heart that divide— God and hate, love and violence—and in this duality the whole culture of man expands and contracts.

The unity of man does not lie in any of the structures which the human mind has invented. Co-operation is not the nature of the intellect. Between love and hate there can be no unity, and yet it is what the mind is trying to find and establish. Unity lies totally outside this field, and thought cannot reach it.

Thought has constructed this culture of aggression, competition and war, and yet this very thought is groping after order and peace. But thought will never find order and peace, do what it will. Thought must be silent for love to be.

6

The mind freeing itself from the known is meditation. Prayer goes from the known to the known; it may produce results, but it is still within the field of the known—and the known is the conflict, the misery and confusion. Meditation is the total denial of everything that the mind has accumulated. The known is the observer, and the observer sees only through the known. The image is of the past, and meditation is the ending of the past.

It was a fairly large room overlooking a garden with many cypresses for a hedge, and beyond it was a monastery, red-roofed. Early in the morning, before the sun rose, there was a light there and you could see the monks moving about. It was a very cold morning. The wind was blowing from the north and the big eucalyptus—towering over every other tree and over the houses—was swaying in the wind most unwillingly. It liked the breezes that came from the sea because they were not too violent; and it took delight in the soft movement of its own beauty. It was there in the morning early and it was there when the sun was setting, catching the evening light, and somehow it conveyed the certainty of nature. It gave assurance to all the trees and bushes and little plants. It must have been a very old tree. But man never looked at it. He would cut it down if necessary to build a house and never feel the loss of it; for in this country trees are not respected and nature has very little place except, perhaps, as a decoration. The magnificent villas with their gardens had trees showing off the graceful curves of the houses. But this eucalyptus was not decorative to any house. It stood by itself, splendidly quiet and full of silent movement; and the monastery with its garden, and the room with its enclosed green space, were within its shadow. It was there, year after year, living in its own dignity.

There were several people in the room. They had come to carry on a conversation which had been started a few days before. They were mostly young people, some with long hair, others with beards, tight trousers, skirts very high, painted lips and piled-up hair.

The conversation began very lightly; they were not quite sure of themselves or where this conversation was going to lead. "Of course we cannot follow the established order," said one of them, "but we are caught in it. What is our relationship with the older generation and their activity?"

Mere revolt is not the answer, is it? Revolt is a reaction, a response which will bring about its own conditioning. Every generation is conditioned by the past generation, and merely to rebel against conditioning does not free the mind which has been conditioned. Any form of obedience is also a resistance which brings about violence. Violence among the students, or the riots in the cities, or war, whether far removed from yourself or within yourself, will in no way bring clarity.

"But how are we to act within the society to which we belong?"

If you act as a reformer then you are patching up society, which is always degenerating, and so sustaining a system which has produced wars, divisions and separativeness. The reformer, really, is a danger to the fundamental change of man. You have to be an outsider to all communities, to all religions and to the morality of society, otherwise you will be caught in the some old pattern, perhaps somewhat modified.

You are an outsider only when you cease to be envious and vicious, cease to worship success or its power motive. To be psychologically an outsider is possible only when you understand yourself who are part of the environment, part of the social structure which you yourself have built—you being the many yous of many thousands of years, the many, many generations that have produced the present. In understanding yourself as a human being you will find your relationship with the older passing generations.

"But how can one be free of the heavy conditioning as a Catholic? It is so deeply ingrained in us, deeply buried in the unconscious."

Whether one is a Catholic, or a Muslim, or Hindu, or a Communist, the propaganda of a hundred, two hundred, or five thousand years is part of this verbal structure of images which goes to make up our consciousness. We are conditioned by what we eat, by the economic pressures, by the culture and society in which we live. We *are* that culture, we *are* that society. Merely to revolt against it is to revolt against ourselves. If you rebel against yourself, not knowing what you are, your rebellion is utterly wasted. But to be aware, without condemnation, of what you are—such awareness brings about action which is entirely different from the action of a reformer or a revolutionary.

"But, sir, our unconscious is the collective racial heritage and according to the analysts this must be understood."

I don't see why you give such importance to the unconscious. It is as trivial and shoddy as the conscious mind, and giving it importance only strengthens it. If you see its true worth it drops away as a leaf in the autumn. We think certain things are important to keep and that others can be thrown away. War does produce certain peripheral improvements, but war itself is the greatest disaster for man. Intellect will in no way solve our human problems. Thought has tried in many, many ways to overcome and go beyond our agonies and anxieties. Thought has built the church, the saviour, the guru; thought has invented nationalities; thought has divided the people in the nation into different communities, classes, at war with each other. Thought has separated man from man, and having brought anarchy and great sorrow, it then proceeds to invent a structure to bring people together. Whatever thought does must inevitably breed danger and anxiety. To call oneself an Italian or an Indian or an American is surely insanity, and it is the work of thought.

"But love is the answer to all this, isn't it?"

Again you're off! Are you free from envy, ambition, or are you merely using that word "love" to which thought has given a meaning? If thought has given a meaning to it, then it is not love. The word love is not love—no matter what you mean by that word. Thought is the past, the memory, the experience, the knowledge from which the response to every challenge comes. So this response is always inadequate, and hence there is conflict. For thought is always old; thought can never be new. Modern art is the response of thought, the intellect, and though it pretends to be new it is really as old, though not as beautiful, as the hills. It is the whole structure built by thought—as love, as God, as culture, as the ideology of the polit-buro—which has to be totally denied for the new to be. The new cannot fit into the old pattern. You are really afraid to deny the old pattern completely.

"Yes, sir, we are afraid, for if we deny it what is there left? With what do we replace it?"

This question is the outcome of thought which sees the danger and so is afraid and wants to be assured that it will find something to replace the old. So again you are caught in the net of thought. But if factually, not verbally or intellectually, you denied this whole house of thought, then you might perhaps find the new—the new way of living, seeing, acting. Negation is the most positive action. To negate the false, not knowing what is true, to negate the apparent truth in the false, and to negate the false as the false, is the instant action of a mind that is free from thought. To see this flower with the image that thought has built about it is entirely different from seeing it without that image. The relationship between the observer and the flower is the image which the observer has about the observed, and in this there is a great distance between them.

When there is no image the time interval ceases.

7

Meditation is always new. It has not the touch of the past for it has no continuity. The word new doesn't convey the quality of a freshness that has not been before. It is like the light of a candle which has been put out and relit. The new light is not the old, though the candle is the same. Meditation has a continuity only when thought colours it, shapes it and gives it a purpose. The purpose and meaning of meditation given by thought becomes a time-binding bondage. But the meditation that is not touched by thought has its own movement, which is not of time. Time implies the old and the new as a movement from the roots of yesterday to the flowing of tomorrow. But meditation is a different flowering altogether. It is not the outcome of the experience of yesterday, and therefore it has no roots at all in time. It has a continuity which is not that of time. The word continuity in meditation is misleading, for that which was, yesterday, is not taking place today. The meditation of today is a new awakening, a new flowering of the beauty of goodness.

The car went slowly through all the traffic of the big town with its buses, lorries and cars, and all the noise along the narrow streets. There were endless flats, filled with families, and endless shops, and the town was spreading on all sides, devouring the countryside. At last we came out into the country, the green fields and the wheat and the great patches of flowering mustard, intense in their yellowness. The contrast between the intense green and the yellow was as striking as the contrast between the noise of the town and the quietness of the countryside. We were on the auto route to the north which went up and down the land. And there were woods, streams, and the lovely blue sky.

It was a spring morning, and there were great patches of bluebells in the wood, and beside the wood was the yellow mustard, stretching almost to the horizon; and then the green wheatfield that stretched as far as the eye could see. The road passed villages and towns, and a side road led to a lovely wood with new fresh spring leaves and the smell of damp earth; and there was that peculiar feeling of spring, and the newness of life. You were very close to nature then as you watched your part of the earth—the trees, the new delicate leaf, and the stream that went by. It was not a romantic feeling or an imaginative sensation, but actually you were all this—the blue sky and the expanding earth.

The road led to an old house with an avenue of tall beeches with their young, fresh leaves, and you looked up through them at the blue sky. It was a lovely morning, and the copper-beech was still quite young, though very tall.

He was a big, heavy man with very large hands, and he

filled that enormous chair. He had a kindly face and he was
ready to laugh. It is strange how little we laugh. Our hearts
are too oppressed, made dull, by the weary business of living,
by the routine and the monotony of everyday life. We are
made to laugh by a joke or a witty saying, but there is no
laughter in ourselves; the bitterness which is man's ripening
fruit seems so common. We never see the running water and
laugh with it; it is sad to see the light in our eyes grow
duller and duller each day; the pressures of agony and despair seem to colour our whole life with their promise of hope
and pleasure, which thought cultivates.

He was interested in that peculiar philosophy of the origin
and acceptance of silence—which probably he had never
come upon. You can't buy silence as you would buy good
cheese. You can't cultivate it as you would a lovely plant.
It doesn't come about by any activity of the mind or of the
heart. The silence that music produces as you listen to it is
the product of that music, induced by it. Silence isn't an
experience; you know it only when it is over.

Sit, sometime, on the bank of a river and look into the
water. Don't be hypnotised by the movement of the water,
by the light, the clarity and the depth of the stream. Look
at it without any movement of thought. The silence is all
round you, in you, in the river, and in those trees that are
utterly still. You can't take it back home, hold it in your
mind or your hand and think you have achieved some extraordinary state. If you have, then it is not silence; then it
is merely a memory, an imagining, a romantic escape from
the daily noise of life.

Because of silence everything exists. The music you heard
this morning came to you out of silence, and you heard it
because you were silent, and it went beyond you in silence.

Only we don't listen to the silence because our ears are
full of the chatter of the mind. When you love, and there is

no silence, thought makes of it a plaything of society whose culture is envy and whose gods are put together by the mind and the hand. Silence is where you are, in yourself and beside yourself.

8

Meditation is the summation of all energy. It is not to be gathered little by little, denying this and denying that, capturing this and holding on to that; but rather, it is the total denial, without any choice, of all wasteful energy. Choice is the outcome of confusion; and the essence of wasted energy is confusion and conflict. To see clearly what is at any time needs the attention of all energy; and in this there is no contradiction or duality. This total energy does not come about through abstinence, through the vows of chastity and poverty, for all determination and action of will is a waste of energy because thought is involved in it, and thought is wasted energy: perception never is. The *seeing* is not a determined effort. There is no "I will see", but only seeing. Observation puts aside the observer, and in this there is no waste of energy. The thinker who attempts to observe, spoils energy. Love is not wasted energy, but when thought makes it into pleasure, then pain dissipates energy. The summation of energy, of meditation, is ever expanding, and action in daily life becomes part of it.

The poplar this morning was being stirred by the breeze that came from the west. Every leaf was telling something to the breeze; every leaf was dancing, restless in its joy of the spring morning. It was very early. The blackbird on the roof was singing. It is there every morning and evening, sometimes sitting quietly looking all around and at other times

calling and waiting for a reply. It would be there for several
minutes and then fly off. Now its yellow beak was bright in
the early light. As it flew away the clouds were coming over
the roof, the horizon was filled with them, one on top of another, as though someone had very carefully arranged them
in neat order. They were moving, and it seemed as if the
whole earth was being carried by them—the chimneys, the
television antennae and the very tall building across the way.
They presently passed, and there was the blue, spring sky,
clear, with the light freshness that only spring can bring. It
was extraordinarily blue and, at that time of the morning,
the street outside was almost silent. You could hear the
noise of heels on the pavement and in the distance a lorry
went by. The day would soon begin. As you looked out of the
window at the poplar you saw the universe, the beauty of it.

He asked: "What is intelligence? You talk a great deal
about it and I would like to know your opinion of it."

Opinion, and the exploration of opinion, is not truth. You
can discuss indefinitely the varieties of opinion, the rightness
and the wrongness of them, but however good and reasonable,
opinion is not the truth. Opinion is always biased, coloured
by the culture, the education, the knowledge which one has.
Why should the mind be burdened with opinions at all,
with what you think about this or that person, or book, or
idea? Why shouldn't the mind be empty? Only when it is
empty can it see clearly.

"But we are all full of opinions. My opinion of the present
political leader has been formed by what he has said and
done, and without that opinion I would not be able to vote
for him. Opinions are necessary for action, aren't they?"

Opinions can be cultivated, sharpened and hardened, and
most actions are based on this principle of like and dislike.
The hardening of experience and knowledge expresses itself

in action, but such action divides and separates man from man; it is opinion and belief that prevent the observation of what actually is. The seeing of *what is* is part of that intelligence which you are asking about. There is no intelligence if there is no sensitivity of the body and of the mind—the sensitivity of feeling and the clarity of observation. Emotionalism and sentimentality prevent the sensitivity of feeling. Being sensitive in one area and dull in another leads to contradiction and conflict—which deny intelligence. The integration of the many broken parts into a whole does not bring about intelligence. Sensitivity is attention, which is intelligence. Intelligence has nothing to do with knowledge or information. Knowledge is always the past; it can be called upon to act in the present but it limits the present. Intelligence is always in the present, and of no time.

9

Meditation is the freeing of the mind from all dishonesty. Thought breeds dishonesty. Thought, in its attempts to be honest, is comparative and therefore dishonest. All comparison is a process of evasion and hence breeds dishonesty. Honesty is not the opposite of dishonesty. Honesty is not a principle. It is not conformity to a pattern, but rather it is the total perception of what is. And meditation is the movement of this honesty in silence.

The day began rather cloudy and dull, and the naked trees were silent in the wood. Through the wood you could see crocuses, daffodils and bright yellow forsythia. You looked at it all from a distance and it was a patch of yellow against a green lawn. As you came close to it you were blinded by the brightness of that yellow—which was God.

It was not that you identified yourself with the colour, or that you became the expanse that filled the universe with yellow—but that there was no you to look at it. Only it existed, and nothing else—not the voices around you, not the blackbird singing its melody of the morning, not the voices of the passers-by, not the noisy car that scraped by you on the road. *It* existed, nothing else. And beauty and love were in that existence.

You walked back into the wood. A few rain drops fell, and the wood was deserted. Spring had just come, but here in the north the trees had no leaves. They were dreary from the winter, from the waiting for sunshine and mild weather. A horseman went by and the horse was sweating. The horse, with its grace, its movement, was more than the man; the man, with his breeches, highly polished boots and riding-cap, looked insignificant. The horse had breeding, it held its head high. The man, although he rode the horse, was a stranger to the world of nature, but the horse seemed part of nature, which man was slowly destroying.

The trees were large—oaks, elms and beeches. They stood very silent. The ground was soft with winter's leaves, and here the earth seemed very old. There were few birds. The blackbird was calling, and the sky was clearing.

When you went back in the evening the sky was very clear and the light on these huge trees was strange and full of silent movement.

Light is an extraordinary thing; the more you watch it the deeper and vaster it becomes; and in its movement the trees were caught. It was startling; no canvas could have caught the beauty of that light. It was more than the light of the setting sun; it was more than your eyes saw. It was as though love was on the land. You saw again that yellow patch of forsythia, and the earth rejoiced.

*   *   *

She came with her two daughters but left them to play outside. She was a young woman, rather nice-looking and quite well dressed; she seemed rather impatient and capable. She said her husband worked in some kind of office, and life went by. She had a peculiar sadness which was covered up with a swift smile. She asked: "What is relationship? I have been married to my husband for some years now. I suppose we love each other—but there is something terribly lacking in it."

You really want to go into this deeply?

"Yes, I have come a long way to talk to you about it."

Your husband works in his office, and you work in your house, both of you with your ambitions, frustrations, agonies and fears. He wants to be a big executive and is afraid that he may not make it—that others may get there before him. He is enclosed in his ambition, his frustration, his search for fulfilment, and you in yours. He comes home tired, irritable, with fear in his heart, and brings home that tension. You also are tired after your long day, with the children, and all the rest of it. You and he take a drink to ease your nerves, and fall into uneasy conversation. After some talk—food, and then the inevitable bed. This is what is called relationship— each one living in his own self-centred activity and meeting in bed; this is called love. Of course, there is a little tenderness, a little consideration, a pat or two on the head for the children. Then there will follow old age and death. This is what is called living. And you accept this way of life.

"What else can one do? We are brought up in it, educated for it. We want security, some of the good things of life. I don't see what else one can do."

Is it the desire for security that binds us? Or is it custom, the acceptance of the pattern of society—the idea of husband, wife and family? Surely in all this there is very little happiness?

"There is some happiness, but there is too much to do, too many things to see to. There is so much to read if one is to be well-informed. There isn't much time to think. Obviously one is not really happy, but one just carries on."

All this is called living in relationship—but obviously there is no relationship at all. You may be physically together for a little while but each one is living in his own world of isolation, breeding his own miseries, and there is no actual coming together, not just physically, but at a much deeper and wider level. It is the fault of society, isn't it, of the culture in which we have been brought up and in which we so easily get caught? It is a rotten society, a corrupt and immoral society which human beings have created. It is this that must be changed, and it cannot be changed unless the human being who has built it changes himself.

"I may perhaps understand what you say, and maybe change, but what of him? It gives him great pleasure to strive, to achieve, to become somebody. He is not going to change, and so we are back again where we were—I, feebly attempting to break through my enclosure, and he more and more strengthening his narrow cell of life. What is the point of it all?"

There is no point in this kind of existence at all. We have made this life, the everyday brutality and ugliness of it, with occasional flashes of delight; so we must die to it all. You know, madam, actually there is no tomorrow. Tomorrow is the invention of thought in order to achieve its shoddy ambitions and fulfilment. Thought builds the many tomorrows, but actually there is no tomorrow. To die tomorrow is to live completely today. When you do, the whole of existence changes. For love is not tomorrow, love is not a thing of thought, love has no past or future. When you live completely today there is a great intensity in it, and in its beauty —which is untouched by ambition, by jealousy or by time—

there is relationship not only with man but with nature, with the flowers, the earth and the heavens. In that there is the intensity of innocence; living, then, has a wholly different meaning.

10

You can never set about to meditate : it must happen without your seeking it out. If you seek it, or ask how to meditate, then the method will not only condition you further but also strengthen your own present conditioning. Meditation, really, is the denial of the whole structure of thought. Thought is structural, reasonable or unreasonable, objective or unhealthy, and when it tries to meditate from reason or from a contradictory and neurotic state it will inevitably project that which it is, and will take its own structure as a serious reality. It is like a believer meditating upon his own belief; he strengthens and sanctifies that which he, out of fear, has created. The word is the picture or the image whose idolatry becomes the end.

Sound makes its own cage, and then the noise of thought is of the cage, and it is this word and its sound which divides the observer and the observed. The word is not only a unit of language, not only a sound, but also a symbol, a recollection of any event which unleases the movement of memory, of thought. Meditation is the complete absence of this word. The root of fear is the machinery of the word.

It was early spring and in the Bois it was strangely gentle. There were few new leaves, and the sky was not yet that intense blue that comes with the delight of spring. The chestnuts were not yet out, but the early smell of spring was in the air. In that part of the Bois there was hardly anybody, and you could hear the cars going by in the distance. We were walking in the early morning and there was that gentle sharpness of the early spring. He had been discussing, questioning, and asking what he should do.

"It seems so endless, this constant analysis, introspective examination, this vigilance. I have tried so many things; the clean-shaven gurus and the bearded gurus, and several systems of meditation—you know the whole bag of tricks—and it leaves one rather dry-mouthed and hollow."

Why don't you begin from the other end, the end you don't know about—from the other shore which you cannot possibly see from this shore? Begin with the unknown rather than with the known, for this constant examination, analysis, only strengthens and further conditions the known. If the mind lives from the other end, then these problems will not exist.

"But how am I to begin from the other end? I don't know it, I can't see it."

When you ask: "How am I to begin from the other end?" you are still asking the question from this end. So don't ask it, but start from the other shore, of which you know nothing, from another dimension which cunning thought cannot capture.

He remained silent for some time, and a cock pheasant flew by. It looked brilliant in the sun, and it disappeared under some bushes. When it reappeared a little later there were four or five hen pheasants almost the colour of the dead leaves, and this big pheasant stood mightily amongst them.

He was so occupied that he never saw the pheasant, and when we pointed it out to him he said: "How beautiful!" —which were mere words, because his mind was occupied with the problem of how to begin from something he didn't know. An early lizard, long and green, was on a rock, sunning itself.

"I can't see how I am going to begin from that end. I

don't really understand this vague assertion, this statement which, at least to me, is quite meaningless. I can go only to what I know."

But what do you know? You know only something which is already finished, which is over. You know only the yesterday, and we are saying: Begin from that which you don't know, and live from there. If you say: "How am I to live from there?" then you are inviting the pattern of yesterday. But if you live with the unknown you are living in freedom, acting from freedom, and, after all, that is love. If you say, "I know what love is", then you don't know what it is. Surely it is not a memory, a remembrance of pleasure. Since it isn't, then live with that which you don't know.

"I really don't know what you are talking about. You are making the problem worse."

I'm asking a very simple thing. I'm saying that the more you dig, the more there is. The very digging is the conditioning, and each shovelful makes steps which lead nowhere. You want new steps made for you, or you want to make your own steps which will lead to a totally different dimension. But if you don't know what that dimension is—actually, not speculatively—then whatever steps you make or tread can lead only to that which is already known. So drop all this and start from the other end. Be silent, and you will find out.

"But I don't know how to be silent!"

There you are, back again in the "how", and there is no end to the how. All knowing is on the wrong side. If you know, you are already in your grave. The being is not the knowing.

II

In the light of silence, all problems are dissolved. This light is not born of the ancient movement of thought. It is not

born, either, out of self-revealing knowledge. It is not lit by
time nor by any action of will. It comes about in meditation.
Meditation is not a private affair; it is not a personal search
for pleasure; pleasure is always separative and dividing. In
meditation the dividing line between you and me disappears;
in it the light of silence destroys the knowledge of the me.
The me can be studied indefinitely, for it varies from day
to day, but its reach is always limited, however extensive it
is thought to be. Silence is freedom, and freedom comes with
the finality of complete order.

It was a wood by the sea. The constant wind had mis-
shapen the pine trees, keeping them short, and the branches
were bare of needles. It was spring, but spring would never
come to these pine trees. It was there, but far away from
them, far away from the constant wind and the salt air. It
was there, flowering, and every blade of grass and every leaf
was shouting, every chestnut tree was in bloom, its candles
lit by the sun. The ducks with their chicks were there, the
tulips and the narcissi. But here it was bare, without shadow,
and every tree was in agony, twisted, stunted, bare. It was
too near the sea. This place had its own quality of beauty
but it looked at those far-away woods with silent anguish,
for that day the cold wind was very strong; there were high
waves and the strong winds drove the spring further inland.
It was foggy over the sea, and the racing clouds covered the
land, carrying with them the canals, the woods and the flat
earth. Even the low tulips, so close to the earth, were shaken
and their brilliant colour was a wave of bright light over the
field. The birds were in the woods, but not among the pines.
There were one or two blackbirds, with their bright yellow
beaks, and a pigeon or two. It was a marvellous thing to see
the light on the water.

*   *   *

He was a big man, heavily built, with large hands. He must have been a very rich man. He collected modern pictures and was rather proud of his collection which the critics had said was very good. As he told you this you could see the light of pride in his eyes. He had a dog, big, active and full of play; it was more alive than its master. It wanted to be out in the grass among the dunes, racing against the wind, but it sat obediently where its master had told it to sit, and soon it went to sleep from boredom.

Possessions possess us more than we possess them. The castle, the house, the pictures, the books, the knowledge, they become far more vital, far more important, than the human being.

He said he had read a great deal, and you could see from the books in the library that he had all the latest authors. He spoke about spiritual mysticism and the craze for drugs that was seeping over the land. He was a rich, successful man, and behind him was emptiness and the shallowness that can never be filled by books, by pictures, or by the knowledge of the trade.

The sadness of life is this—the emptiness that we try to fill with every conceivable trick of the mind. But that emptiness remains. Its sadness is the vain effort to possess. From this attempt comes domination and the assertion of the me, with its empty words and rich memories of things that are gone and never will come back. It is this emptiness and loneliness that isolating thought breeds and keeps nourished by the knowledge it has created.

It is this sadness of vain effort that is destroying man. His thought is not so good as the computer, and he has only the instrument of thought with which to meet the problems of life, so he is destroyed by them. It is this sadness of wasted life which probably he will be aware of only at the moment of his death—and then it will be too late.

So the possessions, the character, the achievements, the domesticated wife, become terribly important, and this sadness drives away love. Either you have one or the other; you cannot have both. One breeds cynicism and bitterness which are the only fruit of man; the other lies beyond all woods and hills.

12

Imagination and thought have no place in meditation. They lead to bondage; and meditation brings freedom. The good and the pleasurable are two different things; the one brings freedom and the other leads to the bondage of time. Meditation is the freedom from time. Time is the observer, the experiencer, the thinker, and time is thought; meditation is the going beyond and above the activities of time.

Imagination is always in the field of time, and however concealed and secretive it may be, it will act. This action of thought will inevitably lead to conflict and to the bondage of time. To meditate is to be innocent of time.

You could see the lake from many miles away. You got to it through winding roads that wandered through fields of grain and the pine forests. It was a very tidy country. The roads were very clean and the farms with their cattle, horses, chickens and pigs were well-ordered. You went through the rolling hills down to the lake, and on every side were mountains covered with snow. It was very clear, and the snow was sparkling in the early morning.

There had been no wars in this country for many centuries, and one felt the great security, the undisturbed routine of everyday life, bringing with it the dullness and indifference of the established society of a good government.

It was a smooth well-kept road, wide enough for cars to

pass each other easily; and now, as you came over the hill, you were among orchards. A little further on there was a great patch of tobacco. As you came near it you could smell the strong smell of ripening tobacco flowers.

That morning, coming down from an altitude, it was beginning to get warm and the air was rather heavy. The peace of the land entered your heart, and you became part of the earth.

It was an early spring day. There was a cool breeze from the north, and the sun was already beginning to make sharp shadows. The tall, heavy eucalyptus was gently swaying against the house, and a single blackbird was singing; you could see it from where you sat. It must have felt rather lonely, for there were very few birds that morning. The sparrows were lined up on the wall overlooking the garden. The garden was rather ill-kept; the lawn needed mowing. The children would come out and play in the afternoon and you could hear their shouts and laughter. They would chase each other among the trees, playing hide-and-seek, and high laughter would fill the air.

There were about eight people around the table at lunch. One was a film director, another a pianist, and there was also a young student from some university. They were talking about politics and the riots in America, and the war that seemed to be going on and on. There was an easy flow of conversation about nothing. The director said, suddenly: "We of the older generation have no place in the coming modern world. A well-known author spoke the other day at the university—and the students tore him to pieces and he was left flat. What he was saying had no relation to what the students wanted, or thought about, or demanded. He was asserting his views, his importance, his way of life, and the students would have none of it. As I know him, I know what he felt. He was really lost, but would not admit it. He wanted to be accepted by the younger generation and they would not have his respectable, traditional way of life—though in his books he wrote about a formalised change. . . . I, personally," went on the director, "see that I have no relation or contact with anyone of the younger generation. I feel that we are hypocrites."

This was said by a man who had many well-known avantgarde films to his name. He was not bitter about it. He was just stating a fact, with a smile and a shrug of his shoulders. What was specially nice about him was his frankness, with that touch of humility which often goes with it.

The pianist was quite young. He had given up his promising career because he thought the whole world of impressarios, concerts, and the publicity and money involved in it, was a glorified racket. He himself wanted to live a different kind of life, a religious life.

He said: "It is the same all the world over. I have just come from India. There the gap between the old and the new is perhaps even wider. There the tradition and the vitality of the old are tremendously strong, and probably the younger generation will be sucked into it. But at least there will be a few, I hope, who will resist and start a different movement.

"And I have noticed, for I have travelled quite a bit, that the younger people (and I am old compared with the young) are breaking away more and more from the establishment. Perhaps they get lost in the world of drugs and oriental mysticism, but they have a promise, a new vitality. They reject the church, the fat priest, the sophisticated hierarchy of the religious world. They don't want to have anything to do with politics or wars. Perhaps out of them will come a germ of the new."

The university student had been silent all this time, eating his spaghetti and looking out of the window; but he was taking in the conversation, as were the others. He was rather shy, and though he disliked study he went to the university and listened to the professors—who couldn't teach him properly. He read a great deal; he liked English literature as well as that of his own country, and had talked about it at other meals and at other times.

He said: "Though I am only twenty I am already old compared with the fifteen-year-olds. Their brains work faster, they are keener, they see things more clearly, they get to the point before I do. They seem to know much more, and I feel old compared with them. But I entirely agree with what you said. You feel you are hypocrites, say one thing and do another. This you can understand in the politicians and in the priests, but what puzzles me is—why should others join this world of hypocrisy? Your morality stinks; you *want* wars.

"As for us, we don't hate the Negro, or the brown man, or any other colour. We feel at home with all of them. I know this because I have moved about with them.

"But you, the older generation, have created this world of racial distinctions and war—and we don't want any of it. So we revolt. But again, this revolt is made fashionable and exploited by the different politicians, and so we lose our original revulsion against all this. Perhaps we, too, will become respectable, moral citizens. But now we hate your morality and have no morality at all."

There was a minute or two of silence; and the eucalyptus was still, almost listening to the words going on around the table. The blackbird had gone, and so had the sparrows.

We said: Bravo, you are perfectly right. To deny all morality is to be moral, for the accepted morality is the morality of respectability, and I'm afraid we all crave to be respected—which is to be recognised as good citizens in a

rotten society. Respectability is very profitable and ensures
you a good job and a steady income. The accepted morality
of greed, envy and hate is the way of the establishment.

When you totally deny all this, not with your lips but with
your heart, then you are really moral. For this morality
springs out of love and not out of any motive of profit, of
achievement, of place in the hierarchy. There cannot be this
love if you belong to a society in which you want to find
fame, recognition, a position. Since there is no love in this,
its morality is immorality. When you deny all this from the
very bottom of your heart, then there is a virtue that is en-
compassed by love.

13

To meditate is to transcend time. Time is the distance that
thought travels in its achievements. The travelling is always
along the old path covered over with a new coating, new
sights, but always the same road, leading nowhere—except
to pain and sorrow.

It is only when the mind transcends time that truth ceases
to be an abstraction. Then bliss is not an idea derived from
pleasure but an actuality that is not verbal.

The emptying of the mind of time is the silence of truth,
and the seeing of this is the doing; so there is no division between the seeing and the doing. In the interval between seeing and doing is born conflict, misery and confusion. That
which has no time is the everlasting.

On every table there were daffodils, young, fresh, just
out of the garden, with the bloom of spring on them still. On
a side table there were lilies, creamy-white with sharp yellow
centres. To see this creamy-white and the brilliant yellow

of those many daffodils was to see the blue sky, ever expanding, limitless, silent.

Almost all the tables were taken by people talking very loudly and laughing. At a table nearby a woman was surreptitiously feeding her dog with the meat she could not eat. They all seemed to have huge helpings, and it was not a pleasant sight to see people eating; perhaps it may be barbarous to eat publicly. A man across the room had filled himself with wine and meat and was just lighting a big cigar, and a look of beatitude came over his fat face. His equally fat wife lit a cigarette. Both of them appeared to be lost to the world.

And there they were, the yellow daffodils, and nobody seemed to care. They were there for decorative purposes that had no meaning at all; and as you watched them their yellow brilliance filled the noisy room. Colour has this strange effect upon the eye. It wasn't so much that the eye absorbed the colour, as that the colour seemed to fill your being. You *were* that colour; you didn't become that colour—you were of it, without identification or name: the anonymity which is innocence. Where there is no anonymity there is violence, in all its different forms.

But you forgot the world, the smoke-filled room, the cruelty of man, and the red, ugly meat; those shapely daffodils seemed to take you beyond all time.

Love is like that. In it there is no time, space or identity. It is the identity that breeds pleasure and pain; it is the identity that brings hate and war and builds a wall around people, around each one, each family and community. Man reaches over the wall to the other man—but he too is enclosed; morality is a word that bridges the two, and so it becomes ugly and vain.

Love isn't like that; it is like that wood across the way, always renewing itself because it is always dying. There is no permanency in it, which thought seeks; it is a movement which thought can never understand, touch or feel. The feeling of thought and the feeling of love are two different things; the one leads to bondage and the other to the flowering of goodness. The flowering is not within the area of any society, of any culture or of any religion, whereas the bondage belongs to all societies, religious beliefs and faith in otherness. Love is anonymous, therefore not violent. Pleasure is violent, for desire and will are moving factors in it. Love cannot be begotten by thought, or by good works. The denial of the total process of thought becomes the beauty of action, which is love. Without this there is no bliss of truth.

And over there, on that table, were the daffodils.

14

Meditation is the awakening of bliss; it is both of the senses and transcending them. It has no continuity, for it is not of time. The happiness and the joy of relationship, the sight of a cloud carrying the earth, and the light of spring on the leaves, are the delight of the eye and of the mind. This delight can be cultivated by thought and given a duration in the space of memory, but it is not the bliss of meditation in which is included the intensity of the senses. The senses must be acute and in no way distorted by thought, by the discipline of conformity and social morality. The freedom of the senses is not the indulgence of them : the indulgence is the pleasure of thought. Thought is like the smoke of a fire and bliss is the fire without the cloud of smoke that brings tears to the eyes. Pleasure is one thing, and bliss another. Pleasure is the bondage of thought, and bliss is beyond and above thought. The foundation of meditation is the understanding of thought and of pleasure, with their morality and the discipline which gives comfort. The bliss of meditation is not of time or duration; it is beyond both and therefore not measurable. Its ecstasy is not in the eye of the beholder, nor is it an experience of the thinker.

Thought cannot touch it with its words and symbols and the confusion it breeds; it is not a word that can take root in thought and be shaped by it. This bliss comes out of complete silence.

It was a lovely morning with fleeting clouds and a clear blue sky. It had rained, and the air was clean. Every leaf was new and the dreary winter was over; each leaf knew, in the sparkling sunshine, that it had no relation to last year's spring. The sun shone through the new leaves, shedding a soft green light on the wet path that led through the woods to the main road that went on to the big city.

There were children playing about, but they never looked at that lovely spring day. They had no need to look, for they were the spring. Their laughter and their play were part of the tree, the leaf and the flower. You felt this, you didn't imagine it. It was as though the leaves and the flowers were taking part in the laughter, in the shouting, and in the balloon that went by. Every blade of grass, and the yellow dandelion, and the tender leaf that was so vulnerable, all were part of the children, and the children were part of the whole earth. The dividing line between man and nature disappeared; but the man on the race-course in his car, and the woman returning from market, were unaware of this. Probably they never even looked at the sky, at the trembling leaf, the white lilac. They were carrying their problems in their hearts, and the heart never looked at the children or at the brightening spring day. The pity of it was that they bred these children and the children would soon become the man on the race-course and the woman returning from the market; and the world would be dark again. Therein lay the unending sorrow. The love on that leaf would be blown away with the coming autumn.

He was a young man with a wife and children. He seemed highly educated, intellectual, and good at the use of words. He was rather lean and sat comfortably in the arm-chair—legs crossed, hands folded on his lap and his glasses sparkling with the light of the sun from the window. He said he had always been seeking—not only philosophical truths but the truth that was beyond the word and the system.

I suppose you are seeking because you are discontented?

"No, I am not exactly discontented. Like every other human being I am dissatisfied, but that's not the reason for the search. It isn't the search of the microscope, or of the telescope, or the search of the priest for his God. I can't say what I'm seeking; I can't put my finger on it. It seems to me I was born with this, and though I am happily married, the search still goes on. It isn't an escape. I really don't know what I want to find. I have talked it over with some clever philosophers and with religious missionaries from the East, and they have all told me to continue in my search and never stop seeking. After all these years it is still a constant disturbance."

Should one seek at all? Seeking is always for something over there on the other bank, in the distance covered by time and long strides. The seeking and the finding are in the future—over there, just beyond the hill. This is the essential meaning of seeking. There is the present and the thing to be found in the future. The present is not fully active and alive and so, of course, that which is beyond the hill is more alluring and demanding. The scientist, if he has his eyes glued to the microscope, will never see the spider on the wall, although the web of his life is not in the microscope but in the life of the present.

"Are you saying, sir, that it is vain to seek; that there is no hope in the future; that all time is in the present?"

All life is in the present, not in the shadow of yesterday or in the brightness of tomorrow's hope. To live in the present one has to be free of the past, and of tomorrow. Nothing is found in the tomorrow, for tomorrow is the present, and yesterday is only a remembrance. So the distance between that which is to be found and that which *is*, is made ever wider by the search—however pleasant and comforting that search may be.

Constantly to seek the purpose of life is one of the odd escapes of man. If he finds what he seeks it will not be worth that pebble on the path. To live in the present the mind must not be divided by the remembrance of yesterday or the bright hope of tomorrow: it must have no tomorrow and no yesterday. This is not a poetic statement but an actual fact. Poesy and imagination have no place in the active present. Not that you deny beauty, but love is that beauty in the present which is not to be found in the seeking.

"I think I'm beginning to see the futility of the years I have spent in the search, in the questions I have asked of myself and of others, and the futility of the answers."

The ending is the beginning, and the beginning is the first step, and the first step is the only step.

15

He was rather a blunt man, full of interest and drive. He had read extensively, and spoke several languages. He had been to the East and knew a little about Indian philosophy, had read the so-called sacred books and had followed some

guru or other. And here he was now, in this little
looking a verdant valley smiling in the morning
snow peaks were sparkling and there were huge
coming over the mountains. It was going to be a very nice
day, and at that altitude the air was clear and the light
penetrating. It was the beginning of summer and there was
still in the air the cold of spring. It was a quiet valley, especially at this time of the year, full of silence, and the sound of
cow-bells, and the smell of pine and new mown grass. There
were a lot of children shouting and playing, and that morning, early, there was delight in the air and the beauty of the
land lay upon one's senses. The eye saw the blue sky and
the green earth, and there was rejoicing.

"Behaviour is righteousness—at least, that's what you have
said. I have listened to you for some years, in different parts
of the world, and I have grasped the teaching. I am not
trying to put that teaching into action in life for then it becomes another pattern, another form of imitation, the acceptance of a new formula. I see the danger of this. I have absorbed a great deal of what you have said and it has almost
become part of me. This may prevent a freedom of action—
upon which you so insist. One's life is never free and spontan-
eous. I have to live my daily life but I'm always watchful
to see that I'm not merely following some new pattern
which I have made for myself. So I seem to lead a double
life; there is the ordinary activity, family, work, and so on,
and on the other hand there is the teaching that you have
been giving, in which I am deeply interested. If I follow the
teaching then I'm the same as any Catholic who conforms
to a dogma. So, from what does one act in daily life if one
lives the teaching without simply conforming to it?"

It is necessary to put aside the teaching and the teacher
and also the follower who is trying to live a different kind of
life. There is only learning: in the learning is the doing. The

ning is not separate from the action. If they are separate, then learning is an idea or a set of ideals according to which action takes place, whereas learning is the doing in which there is no conflict. When this is understood, what is the question? The learning is not an abstraction, an idea, but an actual learning about something. You cannot learn without doing; you cannot learn about yourself except in action. It is not that you first learn about yourself and then act from that knowledge for then that action becomes imitative, conforming to your accumulated knowledge.

"But, sir, every moment I am challenged, by this or by that, and I respond as I always have done—which often means there is conflict. I'd like to understand the pertinence of what you say about learning in these everyday situations."

Challenges must always be new, otherwise they are not challenges, but the response, which is old, is inadequate, and therefore there is conflict. You are asking what there is to learn about this. There is the learning about responses, how they come into being, their background and conditioning, so there is a learning about the whole structure and nature of the response. This learning is not an accumulation from which you are going to respond to the challenge. Learning is a movement not anchored in knowledge. If it is anchored it is not a movement. The machine, the computer, *is* anchored. That is the basic difference between man and the machine. Learning is watching, seeing. If you see from accumulated knowledge then the seeing is limited and there is no new thing in the seeing.

"You say one learns about the whole structure of response. This does seem to mean that there is a certain accumulated volume of what is learnt. On the other hand you say that the learning you speak of is so fluid that it accumulates nothing at all."

Our education is the gathering of a volume of knowledge,

and the computer does this faster and more accurately. What need is there for such an education? The machines are going to take over most of the activities of man. When you say, as people do, that learning is the gathering of a volume of knowledge then you are denying, aren't you, the movement of life, which is relationship and behaviour? If relationship and behaviour are based on previous experience and knowledge, then is there true relationship? Is memory, with all its associations, the true basis of relationship? Memory is images and words, and when you base your relationship on symbols, images and words, can it ever bring about true relationship?

As we said, life is a movement in relationship, and if that relationship is tethered to the past, to memory, its movement is limited and becomes agonising.

"I understand very well what you say, and I ask again, from what do you act? Are you not contradicting yourself when you say that one learns in observing the whole structure of one's responses, and at the same time say that learning precludes accumulation?"

The seeing of the structure is alive, it is moving; but when that seeing adds to the structure then the structure becomes far more important than the seeing, which is the living. In this there is no contradiction. What we are saying is that the seeing is far more important than the nature of the structure. When you give importance to learning about the structure and not to learning as the seeing, then there *is* a contradiction; then seeing is one thing and learning about the structure is another.

You ask, sir, what is the source from which one acts? If there is a source of action then it is memory, knowledge, which is the past. We said the seeing *is* the acting; the two things are not separate. And the seeing is always new and so the acting is always new. Therefore the seeing of the everyday response brings out the new, which is what you call spontaneity. At the very moment of anger there is no recognition of it as anger. The recognition takes place a few seconds later as "being angry". Is this seeing of that anger a choiceless awareness of that anger, or is it again choice based on the old? If it is based on the old, then all the responses to that anger—repression, control, indulgence and so on—are the traditional activity. But when the seeing is choiceless, there is only the new.

From all this arises another interesting problem: our dependence on challenges to keep us awake, to pull us out of our routine, tradition, established order, either through bloodshed, revolt, or some other upheaval.

"Is it possible for the mind not to depend on challenges at all?"

It is possible when the mind is undergoing constant change and has no resting place, safe anchorage, vested interest or commitment. An awakened mind, a mind which is alight— what need has it of challenges of any kind?

16

Meditation is the action of silence. We act out of opinion, conclusion and knowledge, or out of speculative intentions. This inevitably results in contradiction in action between what is and what should be, or what has been. This action out of the past, called knowledge, is mechanical, capable of adjustment and modification but having its roots in the past. And so the shadow of the past always covers the present. Such action in relationship is the outcome of the image, the symbol, the conclusion; relationship then is a thing of the past, and so it is memory and not a living thing. Out of this chatter, disarray and contradiction, activities proceed, breaking up into patterns of culture, communities, social institutions and religious dogmas. From this endless noise, the revolution of a new social order is made to appear as though it really were something new, but as it is from the known to the known it is not a change at all. Change is possible only when denying the known; action then is not according to a pattern but out of an intelligence that is constantly renewing itself.

Intelligence is not discernment and judgment or critical evaluation. Intelligence is the seeing of what is. The what is is constantly changing, and when the seeing is anchored in the past, the intelligence of seeing ceases. Then the dead weight of memory dictates the action and not the intelligence of perception. Meditation is the seeing of all this at a glance. And to see, there must be silence, and from this silence there is action which is entirely different from the activities of thought.

It had been raining all day, and every leaf and every petal was dripping with water. The stream had swollen and the clear water had gone; now it was muddy and fast-running. Only the sparrows were active, and the crows—and the big black-and-white magpies. The mountains were hidden by the clouds, and the low-lying hills were barely visible. It hadn't rained for some days and the smell of fresh rain on dry earth was a delight. If you had been in tropical countries where it doesn't rain for months and every day there is a bright, hot sun which parches the earth, then, when the first rains come, you would smell the fresh rain falling on the old, bare earth, as a delight that enters into the very depths of your heart. But here in Europe there was a different kind of smell, more gentle, not so strong, not so penetrating. It was like a gentle breeze that soon passes away.

The next day there was a clear blue sky early in the

morning; all the clouds were gone, and there was sparkling snow on those mountain peaks, fresh grass in the meadows and a thousand new flowers of the spring. It was a morning full of unutterable beauty; and love was on every blade of grass.

He was a well-known film director and, surprisingly, not at all vain. On the contrary he was very friendly, with a ready smile. He had made many successful pictures, and others were copying them. Like all the more sensitive directors he was concerned with the unconscious, with fantastic dreams, conflicts to be expressed in pictures. He had studied the gods of the analysts and had taken drugs himself for experimental purposes.

The human mind is heavily conditioned by the culture it lives in—by its traditions, by its economic condition, and especially by its religious propaganda. The mind strenuously objects to being a slave to a dictator or to the tyranny of the State, yet willingly submits to the tyranny of the Church or of the Mosque, or of the latest, most fashionable psychiatric dogmas. It cleverly invents—seeing so much helpless misery —a new Holy Ghost or a new Atman which soon becomes the image to be worshipped.

The mind, which has created such havoc in the world, is basically frightened of itself. It is aware of the materialistic outlook of science, its achievements, its increasing domination over the mind, and so it begins to put together a new philosophy; the philosophies of yesterday give place to new theories, but the basic problems of man remain unsolved.

Amidst all this turmoil of war, dissension and utter selfishness, there is the main issue of death. Religions, the very ancient or the recent, have conditioned man to certain dogmas, hopes and beliefs which give a ready-made answer to this issue; but death is not answerable by thought, by the intellect; it is a fact, and you cannot get round it.

You have to die to find what death is, and that, apparently, man cannot do, for he is frightened of dying to everything he knows, to his most intimate, deep-rooted hopes and visions.

There is really no tomorrow, but many tomorrows are between the now of life and the future of death. In this dividing gap man lives, with fear and anxiety, but always keeps an eye on that which is inevitable. He doesn't want even to talk about it, and decorates the grave with all the things he knows.

To die to everything one knows—not to particular forms of knowledge but to all knowing—is death. To invite the future—death—to cover the whole of today is the total dying; then there is no gap between life and death. Then death is living and living is death.

This, apparently, no man is willing to do. Yet man is always seeking the new; always holding in one hand the old and groping with the other into the unknown for the new. So there is the inevitable conflict of duality—the me and the not-me, the observer and the observed, the fact and the what should be.

This turmoil completely ceases when there is the ending of the known. This ending is death. Death is not an idea, a symbol, but a dreadful reality and you cannot possibly escape from it by clinging to the things of today, which are of yesterday, nor by worshipping the symbol of hope.

One has to die to death; only then is innocence born, only then does the timeless new come into being. Love is always new, and the remembrance of love is the death of love.

17

It was a wide, luxuriant meadow with green hills round it. That morning it was brilliant, sparkling with dew, and the birds were singing to the heavens and to the earth. In this meadow with so many flowers, there was a single tree, majestic and alone. It was tall and shapely, and that morning it had a special meaning. It made a long, deep shadow, and between the tree and the shadow there was an extraordinary silence. They were communicating with each other —the reality and the unreality, the symbol and the fact. It was really a splendid tree with its late spring leaves all aflutter in the breeze, healthy, not worm-eaten yet; there was great majesty in it. It wasn't clothed in the robes of majesty but it was in itself splendid and imposing. With the evening it would withdraw into itself, silent and unconcerned, though there might be a gale blowing; and as the sun rose it would wake up too and give out its luxuriant blessing over the meadow, over the hills, over the earth.

The blue jays were calling and the squirrels were very active that morning. The beauty of the tree in its solitude gripped your heart. It wasn't the beauty of what you saw; its beauty lay in itself. Though your eyes had seen more lovely things, it was not the accustomed eye that saw this tree, alone, immense and full of wonder. It must have been very old but you never thought of it as being old. As you went and sat in its shadow, your back against the trunk, you felt the earth, the power in that tree, and its great aloofness. You could almost talk to it and it told you many things. But there was always that sense of its being far away although you touched it and felt its harsh bark which had many ants going up it. This morning its shadow was very sharp and clear and seemed to stretch beyond the hills to other hills. It was really a place of meditation if you know how to meditate. It was very quiet, and your mind, if it was sharp, clear, also became quiet, uninfluenced by the surroundings, a part of that brilliant morning, with the dew still on the grass and on the reeds. There would always be that beauty there, in the meadow with that tree.

He was a middle-aged man, well kept, trim and dressed with good taste. He said he had travelled a great deal though not on any particular business. His father had left him a little money and he had seen a bit of the world, not only what lay upon it but also all those rare things in the very rich museums. He said he liked music and played occasionally. He also seemed well-read. In the course of his conversation, he said: "There's so much violence, anger, and hatred of man against man. We seem to have lost love, to have no beauty in our hearts; probably we have never had it. Love has been made into such a cheap commodity, and artificial beauty has become more important than the beauty of the hills, the trees and the flowers. The beauty of children soon fades. I have been wondering about love and beauty. Do let us talk about it if you can spare a little time."

We were sitting on a bench by a stream. Behind us was a railway line and hills dotted with chalets and farmhouses.

Love and beauty cannot be separated. Without love there is no beauty; they are interlocked, inseparable. We have exercised our minds, our intellect, our cleverness, to such an extent, to such destructiveness, that they predominate, violating what may be called love. Of course, the word is not the real thing at all, any more than that shadow of the tree is the tree. We shan't be able to find out what that love is if we don't step down from our cleverness, our heights of intellectual sophistication, if we don't feel the brilliant water and are not aware of that new grass. Is it possible to find this love in museums, in the ornate beauty of church rituals, in the cinema, or in the face of a woman? Isn't it important for us to find out for ourselves how we have alienated ourselves from the very common things of life? Not that we should neurotically worship nature, but if we lose touch with nature doesn't it also mean that we are losing touch with man, with ourselves? We seek beauty and love outside ourselves, in people, in possessions. They become far more important than love itself. Possessions mean pleasure, and because we hold on to pleasure, love is banished. Beauty is in ourselves, not necessarily in the things about us. When the things about us become more important and we invest beauty in them, then the beauty in ourselves lessens. So more and more, as the world becomes more violent, materialistic, the museums and all those other possessions become the things with which we try to clothe our own nakedness and fill our emptiness.

"Why do you say that when we find beauty in people and in things around us, and when we experience pleasure, it lessens the beauty and the love within us?"

All dependence breeds in us possessiveness, and we become the thing which we possess. I possess this house—I *am* this house. That man on horse-back going by *is* the pride of his possession, though the beauty and dignity of the horse are more significant than the man. So the dependence on the beauty of a line, or on the loveliness of a face, surely must diminish the observer himself; which doesn't mean that we must put away the beauty of a line or the loveliness of a face; it means that when the things outside us become of great meaning, we are inwardly poverty-ridden.

"You are saying that if I respond to that lovely face I am inwardly poor. Yet, if I do not respond to that face or to the line of a building I am isolated and insensitive."

When there is isolation there must, precisely, be dependence, and dependence breeds pleasure, therefore fear. If you don't respond at all, either there is paralysis, indifference, or a sense of despair which has come about through the hopelessness of continual gratification. So we are everlastingly caught in this trap of despair and hope, fear and pleasure, love and hate. When there is inward poverty there is the urge to fill it. This is the bottomless pit of the opposites, the opposites which fill our lives and create the battle of life. All these opposites are identical for they are branches of the same root. Love is not the product of dependence, and love has no opposite.

"Doesn't ugliness exist in the world? And isn't it the opposite of beauty?"

Of course there is ugliness in the world, as hate, violence, and so on. Why do you compare it to beauty, to non-violence? We compare it because we have a scale of values and we put what we call beauty at the top and ugliness at the bottom. Can you not look at violence non-comparatively? And if you do, what happens? You find you are dealing only with facts, not with opinions or with what should be, not with measurements. We can deal with what is and act immediately; what should be becomes an ideology and so is fanciful, and therefore useless. Beauty is not comparable, nor is love, and when you say: "I love this one more than that one", then it ceases to be love.

"To return to what I was saying, being sensitive one responds readily and without complications to the lovely face, to the beautiful vase. This unthinking response slides imperceptibly into dependence and pleasure and all the complications you are describing. Dependence therefore seems to me inevitable."

Is there anything inevitable—except, perhaps, death?

"If it is not inevitable, it means that I can order my conduct, which is therefore mechanical."

The seeing of the inevitable process is to be *not* mechanical. It is the mind that refuses to see what is that becomes mechanical.

"If I see the inevitable, I still wonder where and how to draw the line?"

You don't draw the line, but the seeing brings its own action. When you say, "Where am I to draw the line?" it is the interference of thought which is frightened of being caught and wants to be free. Seeing is not this process of thought; seeing is always new, and fresh, and active. Thinking is always old, never fresh. Seeing and thinking are of two different orders altogether, and these two can never come together. So, love and beauty have no opposites and are not the outcome of inward poverty. Therefore love is at the beginning and not at the end.

18

The sound of the church bells came through the woods across the water and over the deep meadow. The sound was different according to whether it came through the woods or over the open meadows or across the fast-running, noisy stream. Sound, like light has a quality that silence brings; the deeper the silence the more the beauty of the sound is heard. That evening, with the sun riding just above the western hills, the sound of those church bells was quite extraordinary. It was as though you heard the bells for the first time. They were not as old as in the ancient cathedrals but they carried the feeling of that evening. There wasn't a cloud in the sky. It was the longest day of the year, and the sun was setting as far north as it ever would.

We hardly ever listen to the sound of a dog's bark, or to the cry of a child or the laughter of a man as he passes by. We separate ourselves from everything, and then from this isolation look and listen to all things. It is this separation which is so destructive, for in that lies all conflict and confusion. If you listened to the sound of those bells with complete silence you would be riding on it—or, rather, the sound would carry you across the valley and over the hill. The beauty of it is felt only when you and the sound are not separate, when you are part of it. Meditation is the ending of the separation, not by any action of will or desire, or by seeking the pleasure of things not already tasted.

Meditation is not a separate thing from life; it is the very essence of life, the very essence of daily living. To listen to those bells, to hear the laughter of that peasant as he walks by with his wife, to listen to the sound of the bell on the bicycle of the little girl as she passes by: it is the whole of life, and not just a fragment of it, that meditation opens.

"What, to you, is God? In the modern world, among the students, the workers and the politicians, God is dead. For the priests, it is a convenient word to enable them to hang on to their jobs, their vested interests, both physical and spiritual, and for the average man—I don't think it bothers him very much, except occasionally when there is some kind of calamity or when he wants to appear respectable among his respectable neighbours. Otherwise it has very little meaning. So I've made the rather long journey here to find out from you what you believe, or, if you don't like that word, to find out if God exists in your life. I've been to India and visited various teachers in their places there, with their disciples, and they all believe, or more or less maintain, that there *is* God, and point out the way to him. I would like, if I may, to talk over with you this rather important question which has haunted man for many thousands of years."

Belief is one thing, reality another. One leads to bondage and the other is possible only in freedom. The two have no relationship. Belief cannot be abandoned or set aside in order to get that freedom. Freedom is not a reward, it is

not the carrot in front of the donkey. It is important from
the beginning to understand this—the contradiction between
belief and reality.

Belief can never lead to reality. Belief is the result of conditioning, or the outcome of fear, or the result of an outer
or inner authority which gives comfort. Reality is none of
these. It is something wholly different, and there is no pas-
sage from this to that. The theologian starts from a fixed
position. He believes in God, in a Saviour, or in Krishna
or in Christ, and then spins theories according to his conditioning and the cleverness of his mind. He is, like the
Communist theoretician, tied to a concept, a formula, and
what he spins is the outcome of his own deliberations.

The unwary are caught in this, as the unwary fly is
caught in the web of the spider. Belief is born out of fear
or tradition. Two thousand or ten thousand years of propaganda is the religious structure of words, with the rituals,
dogmas and beliefs. The word, then, becomes extremely important, and the repetition of that word mesmerises the
credulous. The credulous are always willing to believe,
accept, obey, whether what is offered is good or bad, mis-
chievous or beneficial. The believing mind is not an enquiring mind, and so it remains within the limits of the formula
or the principle. It is like an animal who, tied to a post,
can wander only within the limits of the rope.

"But without belief we have nothing! I believe in goodness; I believe in holy matrimony; I believe in the here-
after and in evolutionary growth towards perfection. To me
these beliefs are immensely important for they keep me in
line, in morality; if you take away belief I am lost."

Being good, and becoming good, are two different things.
The flowering of goodness is not becoming good. Becoming
good is the denial of goodness. Becoming better is a denial
of what is; the better corrupts the what is. Being good is

now, in the present; becoming good is in the future, which is the invention of the mind that is caught in belief, in a formula of comparison and time. When there is measurement, the good ceases.

What is important is not *what* you believe, what your formulas, principles, dogmas and opinions are, but why you have them at all, why your mind is burdened with them. Are they essential? If you put that question to yourself seriously you will find that they are the result of fear, or of the habit of accepting. It is this basic fear which prevents you being involved in what actually *is*. It is this fear that makes for commitment. Being involved is natural; you are involved in life, in your activities; you are *in* life, in the whole movement of it. But to be committed is a deliberate action of a mind that functions and thinks in fragments; one is committed only to a fragment. You cannot deliberately commit yourself to what you consider the whole because this consideration is part of a process of thought, and thought is always separative, it always functions in fragments.

"Yes, you cannot be committed without naming that to which you are committed, and naming is limiting."

Is that statement of yours merely a series of words or an actuality which you have now realised? If it is merely a series of words then it is a belief and therefore has no value at all. If it is an actual truth that you have now discovered, then you are free and in negation. The negation of the false is not a statement. All propaganda is false, and man has lived on propaganda ranging from soap to God.

"You are forcing me into a corner by your perception, and isn't this also a form of propaganda—to propagate what *you* see?"

Surely not. You are forcing *yourself* into a corner where you have to face things as they are, unpersuaded, uninfluenced. You are beginning to realise for yourself what is actually in front of you, therefore you are free of another, free of all authority—of the word, of the person, of the idea. To *see*, belief is not necessary. On the contrary, to see, the absence of belief is necessary. You can see only when there is a negative state, not the positive state of a belief. Seeing is a negative state in which the "what is" is alone evident. Belief is a formula of inaction which breeds hypocrisy, and it is this hypocrisy against which all the younger generation are fighting and revolting. But the younger generation get caught in that hypocrisy later on in life. Belief is a danger which must be totally avoided if one is to see the truth of what is. The politician, the priest, the respectable, will always function according to a formula, forcing others to live according to that formula, and the thoughtless, the foolish, are always blinded by their words, their promises, their hopes. The authority of the formula becomes far more important than the love of what is. Therefore authority is evil, whether it be the authority of belief, or of tradition, or of the custom which is called morality.

"Can I be free of this fear?"

Surely you're putting a wrong question, aren't you? You *are* the fear; you and the fear are not two separate things. The separation is fear which breeds the formula that "I will conquer it, suppress it, escape from it". This is the tradition which gives a false hope of overcoming fear. When you see that you *are* the fear, that you and fear are not two separate things, fear disappears. Then formulas and beliefs are not necessary at all. Then you live only with what is, and see the truth of it.

"But you've not answered the question about God, have you?"

Go to any place of worship—is God there? In the stone, in the word, in the ritual, in the stimulated feeling of seeing something beautifully done? Religions have divided God as yours and mine, the Gods of the East and the Gods of the West, and each God has killed the other God. Where is God to be found? Under a leaf, in the skies, in your heart, or, is it merely a word, a symbol, representing something that cannot be put into words? Obviously you must put aside the symbol, the place of worship, the web of words that man has woven around himself. Only after having done this, not before, can you begin to enquire if there is or is not a reality which is immeasurable.

"But when you have discarded all this you are completely lost, empty, alone—and in this state how can you enquire?"

You are in this state because you are pitying yourself, and self-pity is an abomination. You are in this state because you have not seen, actually, that the false *is* the false. When you see it, it gives you tremendous energy and freedom to see the truth as the truth, not as an illusion or a fancy of the mind. It is this freedom that is necessary from which to see if there is or is not something which cannot be put into words. But it is not an experience, a personal achievement. All experiences, in this sense, bring about a separative, contradictory existence. It is this separative existence as the thinker, the observer, that demands further and wider experiences, and what he demands he will have—but it is not the truth.

Truth is not yours or mine. What is yours can be organised, enshrined, exploited. That is what is happening in the world. But truth cannot be organised. Like beauty and love, truth is not in the realm of possessions.

19

If you walk through the little town with its one street of

many shops—the baker, the camera shop, the bookshop and the open restaurant—under the bridge, past the couturier, over another bridge, past the sawmill, then enter the wood and continue along by the stream, looking at all the things you have passed, with your eyes and all your senses fully awake, but without a single thought in your mind—then you will know what it means to be without separation. You follow that stream for a mile or two—again without a single flutter of thought—looking at the rushing water, listening to its noise, seeing the colour of it, the grey-green mountain stream, looking at the trees and the blue sky through the branches, and at the green leaves—again without a single thought, without a single word—then you will know what it means to have no space between you and the blade of grass.

If you pass on through the meadows with their thousand flowers of every colour imaginable, from bright red to yellow and purple, and their bright green grass washed clean by last night's rain, rich and verdant—again without a single movement of the machinery of thought—then you will know what love is. To look at the blue sky, the high full-blown clouds, the green hills with their clear lines against the sky, the rich grass and the fading flower—to look without a word of yesterday; then, when the mind is completely quiet, silent, undisturbed by any thought, when the observer is completely absent—then there is unity. Not that you are united with the flower, or with the cloud, or with those sweeping hills; rather there is a feeling of complete non-being in which the division between you and another ceases. The woman carrying those provisions which she bought in the market, the big black Alsatian dog, the two children playing with the ball—if you can look at all these without a word, without a measure, without any association, then the quarrel between you and another ceases. This state, without the word, without thought, is the expanse of mind that has no boundaries, no frontiers within which the I and the not-I can exist. Don't think this is imagination, or some flight of fancy, or some desired mystical experience; it is not. It is as actual as the bee on that flower or the little girl on her bicycle or the man going up the ladder to paint the house—the whole conflict of the mind in its separation has come to an end. You look without the look of the observer, you look without the value of the word and the measurement of yesterday. The look of love is different from the look of thought. The one leads in a direction where thought cannot follow, and the other leads to separation, conflict and sorrow. From this sorrow you cannot go to the other. The distance between the two is made by thought, and thought cannot by any stride reach the other.

As you walk back by the little farmhouses, the meadows and the railway line, you will see that yesterday has come to an end : life begins where thought ends.

"Why is it I cannot be honest?" she asked. "Naturally, I am dishonest. Not that I want to be, but it slips out of me. I say things I don't really mean. I'm not talking about polite conversation about nothing—then one knows that one is talking just for the sake of talking. But even when I'm serious I find myself saying things, doing things, that are absurdly dishonest. I've noticed it with my husband too. He says one thing and does something entirely different. He promises, but you know so well that while he is saying it he doesn't quite mean it; and when you point it out to him he gets irritated, sometimes very angry. We both know we are dishonest in so many things. The other day he made a promise to somebody whom he rather respected, and that man went away believing my husband. But my husband didn't keep his word and he found excuses to prove that he was right and the other man wrong. You know the game we play with ourselves and with others—it is part of our social structure and relationship. Sometimes it reaches the point where it becomes very ugly and deeply disturbing—and I have come to that state. I am greatly disturbed, not only about my husband but about myself and all those people who say one thing and do something else and think something else again. The politician makes promises and one knows exactly what his promises mean. He promises heaven on earth and you know very well he's going to create hell on earth—and he will blame it all on factors beyond his control. Why is it that one is so basically dishonest?"

What does honesty mean? Can there be honesty—that is, clear insight, seeing things as they are—if there is a principle, an ideal, an ennobled formula? Can one be direct if there is confusion? Can there be beauty if there is the standard of what is beautiful or upright? When there is this division between what is and what should be, can there be honesty—or only an edifying and respectable dishonesty? We are brought up between the two—between what actually is and what may be. In the interval between these two—the interval of time and space—is all our education, our morality, our struggle. We keep a distracted look upon the one and upon the other, a look of fear and a look of hope. And can there be honesty, sincerity, in this state, which society calls education? When we say we are dishonest, essentially we mean there is a comparison between what we have said and what is. One has said something which one doesn't mean, perhaps to give passing assurance or because one is nervous, shy or ashamed to say something which actually *is*. So nervous apprehension and fear make us dishonest. When we are pursuing success we must be somewhat dishonest, play up to another, be cunning, deceitful, to achieve our end. Or one has gained authority or a position which one wants to defend. So all resistance, all defence, is a form of dishonesty. To be honest means to have no illusions about oneself and no seed of illusion—which is desire and pleasure.

"You mean to say that desire breeds illusion! I desire a nice house—there isn't any illusion in that. I desire my husband to have a better position—I can't see illusion in that either!"

In desire there is always the better, the bigger, the more. In desire there is the measurement, the comparison—and the root of illusion is comparison. The good is not the better, and all our life is spent pursuing the better—whether it be the better bathroom, or the better position, or the better god. Discontent with what is makes the change in what is—which is merely the improved continuity of what is. Improvement is not change, and it is this constant improvement—both in ourselves and in the social morality—which breeds dishonesty.

"I don't know if I follow you, and I don't know if I want to follow you," she said with a smile. "I understand verbally what you say, but where are you leading? I find it rather frightening. If I lived, actually, what you are saying, probably my husband would lose his job, for in the business world there is a great deal of dishonesty. Our children, too, are brought up to compete, to fight to survive. And when I realise, from what you are saying, that we are training them to be dishonest—not obviously, of course, but in subtle and devious ways—then I get frightened for them. How can they face the world, which is so dishonest and brutal, unless they themselves have some of this dishonesty and brutality? Oh, I know I'm saying dreadful things, but there it is! I'm beginning to see how utterly dishonest I am!"

To live without a principle, without an ideal, is to live facing that which is every minute. The actual facing of what is—which is to be completely in contact with it, not through the word or through past associations and memories, but directly in touch with it—is to be honest. To know you have lied and make no excuse for it but to see the actual fact of it, *is* honesty; and in this honesty there is great beauty. The beauty does not hurt anybody. To say one is a liar is an acknowledgement of the fact; it is to acknowledge a mistake as a mistake. But to find reasons, excuses and justifications for it is dishonesty, and in this there is self-pity. Self-pity is the darkness of dishonesty. It does not mean that one must become ruthless with oneself, but rather, one is attentive. To be attentive means to care, to look.

"I certainly did not expect all this when I came. I felt rather ashamed of my dishonesty and didn't know what to do about it. The incapacity to do anything about it made me feel guilty, and fighting guilt or resisting it brings in other problems. Now I must carefully think over everything you have said."

If I may make a suggestion, don't think it over. See it now as it is. From that seeing something new will happen. But if you think it over you are back again in the same old trap.

20

In the animal, the instincts to follow and to obey are natural and necessary for survival, but in man they become a danger. To follow and obey, in the individual, becomes imitation, conformity to a pattern of society which he himself has built. Without freedom, intelligence cannot function. To understand the nature of obedience and acceptance in action brings freedom. Freedom is not the instinct to do what one wants. In a vast complex society that isn't possible; hence the conflict between the individual and society, between the many and the one.

It had been very hot for days; the heat was stifling and at

this altitude the sun's rays penetrated every pore of your body and made you rather dizzy. The snow was melting rapidly and the stream became more and more brown. The big waterfall cascaded in torrents. It came from a large glacier, perhaps more than a kilometre long. This stream would never be dry.

That evening the weather broke. The clouds were piling up against the mountains and there were crashes of thunder, and lightning, and it began to rain; you could smell the rain.

There were three or four of them in that little room overlooking the river. They had come from different parts of the world and they seemed to have a common question. The question was not so important as their own state. Their own state of mind conveyed much more than the question. The question was like a door which opened into a house of many rooms. They were not a very healthy lot, and unhappy in their own way. They were educated—whatever that may mean; they spoke several languages, and appeared ill-kempt.

"Why should one not take drugs? You apparently seem to be against it. Your own prominent friends have taken them, have written books about them, encouraged others to take them, and they have experienced with great intensity the beauty of a simple flower. We, too, have taken them and we would like to know why you seem to be opposed to these chemical experiences. After all, our whole physical organism is a bio-chemical process, and adding to it an extra chemical may give us an experience which may be an approximation to the real. You yourself have not taken drugs, have you? So how can you, without experimenting, condemn them?"

No, we have not taken drugs. Must one get drunk to know what sobriety is? Must one make oneself ill to find out what health is? As there are several things involved in taking drugs, let us go into the whole question with care. What is the

necessity of taking drugs at all—drugs that promise a psyche-
delic expansion of the mind, great visions and intensity?
Apparently one takes them because one's own perceptions are
dull. Clarity is dimmed and one's life is rather shallow,
mediocre and meaningless; one takes them to go beyond this
mediocrity.

The intellectuals have made of the drugs a new way of
life. One sees throughout the world the discord, the neurotic
compulsions, the conflicts, the aching misery of life. One is
aware of the aggressiveness of man, his brutality, his utter
selfishness, which no religion, no law, no social morality has
been able to tame.

There is so much anarchy in man—and such scientific
capacities. This imbalance brings about havoc in the world.
The unbridgable gap between advanced technology and the
cruelty of man is producing great chaos and misery. This is
obvious. So the intellectual, who has played with various
theories—Vedanta, Zen, Communist ideals, and so on—having found no way out of man's predicament, is now turning
to the golden drug that will bring about dynamic sanity and
harmony. The discovery of this golden drug—the complete
answer to everything—is expected of the scientist and probably he will produce it. And the authors and the intellectuals
will advocate it to stop all wars, as yesterday they advocated
Communism or Fascism.

But the mind, with its extraordinary capacities for scientific
discoveries and their implementation, is still petty, narrow
and bigoted, and will surely continue, will it not, in its
pettiness? You may have a tremendous and explosive experience through one of these drugs, but will the deep-rooted
aggression, bestiality and sorrow of man disappear? If these
drugs can solve the intricate and complex problems of relationship, then there is nothing more to be said, for then
relationship, the demand for truth, the ending of sorrow, are

all a very superficial affair to be resolved by taking a pinch of the new golden drug.

Surely this is a false approach, isn't it? It is said that these drugs give an experience approximating to reality, therefore they give hope and encouragement. But the shadow is not the real; the symbol is never the fact. As is observed throughout the world, the symbol is worshipped and not the truth. So isn't it a phoney assertion to say that the result of these drugs is near the truth?

No dynamic golden pill is ever going to solve our human problems. They can be solved only by bringing about a radical revolution in the mind and the heart of man. This demands hard, constant work, seeing and listening, and thus being highly sensitive.

The highest form of sensitivity is the highest intelligence, and no drug ever invented by man will give this intelligence. Without this intelligence there is no love; and love is relationship. Without this love there is no dynamic balance in man. This love cannot be given—by the priests or their gods, by the philosophers, or by the golden drug.